Endorsements

Paul and Arlene Samuels' beautiful, powerful book is timely and desperately needed. The Samuels brilliantly share the real-life stories, struggles, and successes of others from every background and age who live with all forms of mental illness. They also share their own personal experiences with Paul having bipolar and Arlene as his loving support person. While millions of people live with mental illnesses, each person is unique. *Mental Health Meltdown* will help countless people, surfacing every emotion, then leaving us with hope, encouragement, and peace.

—Kathy Ireland, Co-Founder, Kathy Ireland Worldwide
Executive Producer, Anxious Nation

Mental Health Meltdown is an incredibly important resource for those who feel as though they are lost, hopeless, or alone in their struggle. When we share our journey, we not only heal ourselves but others as well. I feel at peace knowing that there are others, like those in this book, who understand.

—Jonny McCoy, Founder, WhiteFlag App

Insightful and moving, the Samuels have gathered first-person stories that challenge preconceptions while enlightening readers' minds and changing hearts. As a professor, I observe that stigmas are a societal problem. Amplifying voices in this groundbreaking book will help to address what I call "inequitable compassion," a sad reality that mental health illnesses are not understood or treated with the same degree of compassion as physical ailments. Academia must create a learning environment that welcomes students grappling with these issues. A ray of sunshine, *Mental*

Health Meltdown encourages us to pay attention, gain knowledge, and make the world a better place for us all.

—Dr. Ray A. Snyder, LHD, Business Professor
Trident Technical College, Charleston, SC,
AACC 2019 Educator of the Year for Southern United States

Paul Samuels' writings are from the heart. He is a great example of how God never wastes a hurt. Paul took the thorn in his flesh (bipolar disorder) and turned it into a platform for ministry and healing. He and his wife, Arlene, have learned to practice gratitude and faith in their hard seasons, proclaiming the hope that is found in God and community. Their authentic stories come from experience and serve as a ray of light in the darkness that mental illness can bring.

—Barbara Jarratt, LPC,
Ministry Assistant, CRM, Pastoral Care Ministry johnsonferry.org

Many families today are impacted by mental health challenges in the life of a loved one. Paul and Arlene Samuels have personally experienced the struggles of bipolar disorder. They have learned to not just survive but thrive! The transparency and vulnerability with which they share their challenges and victories are helpful to me—and will be to you!

—Kirk Humphreys, Former Mayor of Oklahoma City (1998-2003),
Board Chairman, PULSE Evangelism

As president and CEO of Concerned Women for America, my attention is on the well-being of women. CWA, the largest public policy group for women in America, gives me a front row seat, watching with alarm the growing trauma and mental health issues among women. My own childhood with a mom who struggled with clinical depression and suicidal ideation has left me with indelible scars but great hope in Jesus Christ. Co-authored by Arlene and Paul Samuels, their hearts respond to helping others.

The book is an inspiring, revealing collection of first-person stories from those with mental illness in all walks of life. Help and encouragement fill the easy-to-read pages.

—Penny Young Nance, CEO and President,
Concerned Women for America

As a film producer and advocate for many years, I have often traveled to Israel. I have visited Israel twice since the October 7, 2023, war began. In many conversations with both Jewish and Christian citizens, their traumas are evident and will last a long time. This book's first-person stories will likewise give readers anywhere hope for the mental health challenges they face!

—Rev. Mark Jenkins
Former U.S. Representative, the Christian Desk of Yad Vashem,
Israel's official memorial to the victims of the Holocaust

Arlene Bridges Samuels is a voice for the voiceless. From her passion and support for Israel to advocating for those suffering from mental illness, she always puts the interests of others first. Her wisdom and insight come from her love of others and desire to help.

—Alan Keck-Mayor, Somerset, Kentucky

It is my high honor and privilege to endorse this book by Paul Samuels, a veteran of the US Navy. As a chaplain for the Disabled American Veterans, I have ministered to veterans who are bipolar. A book defining the disorder has been much needed in the veteran community. I am so glad Paul has written it.

—Rev. Robert J. Plowman, Chaplain, DAV

Many churches do not know how to help those suffering from mental illness. Your book will help change perceptions. Anne and I admire your courage, Paul, in not only managing your bipolar but sharing your memoir in *Bipolar Missionary*. We cannot think of a better team than you and Arlene to write this book to educate the public by sharing the stories of others.

—Rev. Jim and Anne Bevis, President, CSR Ministries
WGBT Radio "What on Earth Is God Doing?"

My personal friends, Paul and Arlene Samuels, have written a valuable book for our culture. As a senior pastor to thousands from North Carolina to Southern California and internationally in social media, I recommend reading and sharing their book with your family and friends! They will be glad you did, and you will be blessed. The stories in *Mental Health Meltdown* echo Proverbs 25:11 (NKJV): "A word fitly spoken is like apples of gold in settings of silver."

—Dr. Tony Crisp, PhD, Corporate Pastor,
5 Stones Intelligence and Co-Founder, Warriors-Walk

For years, I have watched this couple's firm determination with a bipolar diagnosis in their path. They have borne their book as a team, embracing obstacles as steppingstones. Desiring to help others led them to gather stories of others—and theirs—to find strength and solace in our struggles.

—Doris Mintz, Chairman and Founding Member, Maasay Yahdav

Paul and Arlene Samuels' book, *Mental Health Meltdown*, is a must-read to gain a deeper understanding of mental illness and learn how to support those living with it. I was deeply touched by the bravery and resilience of the storytellers themselves. The stories of friends and families were equally powerful. Their insights will lift the shadow of stigmas and offer glimmers of hope for a brighter future.

—Arlette Revells, CEO, Great Works Creation Co.

Paul's memoir, *Bipolar Missionary*, written in 2020, was his first step in educating others about mental illness. I'm excited that Arlene, an accomplished writer, is co-authoring *Mental Health Meltdown*. Its collection of powerful stories from those struggling with mental illnesses is an education and inspiration for communities across America where mental illness is increasing.

—Wanda Howard, CEO Entrepreneur

The reality of mental illness is never sufficiently discussed, and its impact can never sufficiently be measured. It is a sad reality that needs to be explored and exposed. In *Mental Health Meltdown*, Paul and Arlene Bridges Samuels share their important voices and those of others on a topic that can and must be discussed openly and can never be explored and exposed enough.

—Jonathan Feldstein, President, Genesis 123 Foundation

As a professional who understands the importance of advancing mental health awareness and destigmatization, I'm thrilled to endorse *Mental Health Meltdown*. Understanding these conditions is crucial in fostering empathy, support, and effective treatment strategies. I applaud the authors' dedication to shedding light on these important issues and believe their book will be instrumental in fostering greater understanding and compassion.

—Dr. Steve Lako, D.C.

With empathy and grace, *Mental Health Meltdown* delves into the unique struggles and triumphs experienced in mental illnesses. Paul and Arlene shed light on the often-overlooked complexities of mental illness for believers trying to pursue a Christian life *and* those of other faiths. They provide hard-earned lessons for those with or without mental illness to cultivate resilience matched with understanding. Their book is a gift of encouragement to all who walk similar paths as Paul, with bipolar, and

Arlene, his devoted wife. These stories prompt radical empathy for those fighting mental health battles.

—Shelley Neese, President, the Jerusalem Connection,
Author of *Bible Fiber*

Mental Health Meltdown connects my passion for Israel and Gen Z as a Christ-follower and advocate. I am deeply concerned for our Jewish sisters and brothers in their terrible traumas since October 7, 2023, and about Gen Z, a promising generation facing a rise in depression and anxiety disorders. The Samuels' book, written with hearts of love, is inspiring and easy to read, a tool to help others navigate mental health meltdowns.

—Leah Miles, Co-Founder, Christian Women for Israel
and Senior Director, Donor Ministries for Pulse Evangelism

I highly recommend Paul and Arlene's inspiring book to anyone and their families dealing with mental illness difficulties. My older brother fought paranoid schizophrenia for more than fifty years. The journey was full of ups and downs … mostly downs. Thankfully, our family knew the Lord stood beside us. I cherish the Samuels' friendship. As overcomers, with Paul's bipolar disorder and Arlene by his side, they are role models in daily battles. I am confident the first-person stories will heal many.

—Pastor Chris Edmonds, CEO Roddie's Code
Author of *No Surrender*

We take great joy as part of the prayer support team for our dear friends, Paul and Arlene, in their creative project, which will bless many. Their journey through the years dealing with the effects of bipolar gives them the authority and compassion to compile *Mental Health Meltdown*.

—Jeff and Jean Nease, Member Care with
Youth With A Mission since 1998

Arlene and Paul Samuels speak up about mental illnesses in their co-authored book. Indubitably, their resilience through the years has blessed many with words of hope for those of us who have similar challenges. Their words move us away from dwelling on the past and redirect us to a promising future.

—The Reverend Dr. B. Mike Alexander Jr.,
Retired South Carolina United Methodist clergy

HELPING YOU HOLD ON TO HOPE

Mental Health Meltdown

illuminating the voices of bipolar
and other mental illnesses

Shalom!

Paul Leon Samuels

Paul Leon Samuels &
Arlene Bridges Samuels

Arlene Bridges Samuels

HIGHERLIFE
PUBLISHING & MARKETING

HigherLife Development Services, Inc.,
PO Box 623307
Oviedo, FL 32762
(407) 563-4806
higherlifepublishing.com

Published 2024

Printed in the United States of America

30 29 28 27 26 25 24 1 2 3 4 5

ISBN: 978-1-964081-03-8 (paperback)
ISBN: 978-1-964081-04-5 (ebook)
Copyright Case Number: 2024909216

Dedication

Our heartfelt thanks to our storytellers who courageously shared your insights and to all who love and support you. Immeasurable thanks to Kathie Maier Rodkey for wisely mentoring Paul during the book's process and providing important case studies from her books.

Wanda Howard has championed our book in ways beyond measure, and others who have graciously responded with financial support, prayers, or endorsements. You have amplified our ministry of hope to touch those who suffer with invisible heartaches.

The beautiful sunrise gracing our front cover was photographed by our long-time friend, Ned McNair, on Hilton Head Island, South Carolina. Thank you, *Mr. Sunrise*.

My bride of forty-eight years has been the love of my life since the moment I met her. Arlene is a brilliant beauty, inside and out, remarkable, multi-talented, and devoted in what the Bible describes as "a noble wife of character."

Our two adult children walked with us through the painful years before Dad's diagnosis. You strengthened us to write within the outpouring of your love, forgiveness, and patience.

Paul's generosity, servant's heart, sense of humor, intellect, and enduring persistence to overcome are hallmarks of his life. We remain humbled by God's rescue missions into our brokenness and His jewels of joy scattered along our path with undeserved favor.

Contents

Foreword

Our society is facing a historic need to skillfully address our nation's mental health crisis. Our national mental health reality must change into a mandate to rehabilitate our system for the sake of our citizens. The statistics are alarming. The National Alliance on Mental Illness (NAMI) reports that annually, one in five adults experience mental illness, with one in twenty of them considered serious. Among our youth, one in six (ages six to seventeen) have mental health issues each year, with 50 percent beginning by age fourteen and 75 percent by age twenty-four. Suicide is a shocking reality for our youth and our soldiers. Our current structures and staff are simply not enough. Previously, most states had large mental health institutions. Sadly, all were closed due to a lack of interest in the mentally ill and the financial expenditures to provide help. My own history is decades-long, entering the mental health system as a deeply traumatized six-year-old who witnessed terrible events that shattered my family. The obstacles are enormous, and although attention and solutions are growing by adding professionals, books, and facilities, we must quickly move forward. Mental health emergencies are bursting into all age groups. Authors like Paul and Arlene, who are opening compassionate conversations, are part of valuable input and venues from every sector working together on our national crisis. *Mental Health Meltdown* persuades us to help others hold on to hope. Let us act now to make that happen!

—Kathie Maier Rodkey, Author of *A Layperson's Guide to Living with Mental Disease, Free to Be Insane, The Bin of Life, The Customer Isn't Always Right,* and *A Grandparent's Guide*

Preface

Why in the world would a retired senior couple decide to author a book about mental health after enjoying a full life of career, family and friends? Honestly, we had to. After years learning to live with a mental illness and with mental health shadows now hovering over our world, we were compelled to introduce you to stories of those who are surviving, even thriving despite the mental health challenges they face. We wanted to help others hold on to hope too!

With June birthdays two years and two days apart, 1944 and 1946, we are surprised that we have lived this long. We could not be more different and more alike even if we had written every word of our own life scripts and marriage. Like one of our favorite theme songs, a 1927 popular song called Side by Side, "we've traveled our road, sharing our load." Exploring out-of-the-box creative ideas and solutions to the mental health challenges we have personally faced is something we have learned to do. But we are not alone. We have met so many others who have a unique and inspiring story to share. That's what this book is all about.

When we determined to co-author *Mental Health Meltdown*, our lives took another unexpected, yet exciting turn; this time here at home yet still with our international outlook based on our experiences, travels, and professions. With Paul having bipolar, this book is part of our family story. We both are committed to reaching out to others with insight and information that will bring hope and courage.

This book is for anyone who either struggles with a mental illness or knows or cares for someone who does. It doesn't matter your age, ethnicity, or faith. We believe the stories in this book will help you navigate within the complex tapestry of mental illnesses.

Paul loves to tell others that I have a master's degree in Rehabilitation Counseling from the University of Alabama. With a big smile he adds, "I could be Arlene's PhD." *Mental Health Meltdown* is truly our shared PhD, one that we pray will help you, family, and friends hold on to hope!

Prologue

"When a train goes through a tunnel and it gets dark, you don't throw away the ticket and jump off. You sit still and trust the engineer."
—*Dutch Author Corrie ten Boom*

Our book features brave storytellers who share their journeys with bipolar and other mental illnesses, accompanied by stories from their friends and families. They have faced dark tunnels while living in a culture that often perceives them as those who may never see the light ahead. Our book is a traveling companion through the darkness, piercing it with the hope of reducing stigmas by adding insights through these pages.

Mental illness lives in the shadows of conversation, often discussed only in whispers. The presence of bipolar, clinical depression, PTSD, and other differently wired brains traps folks into silence. Fearing rejection, shame, and stigmas affects not only those of us *with* a mental illness but also how we are viewed by people who do not have mental illness. Hearts and minds open when conversations take place with kindness and safety. Just as no one chooses a lifetime of physical disability, no one chooses to have a mental illness. Stepping into the light, those with brain disorders educate others and help compel cultural changes. An equality of understanding and acceptance emerges for those with mental or physical challenges.

We invite you to ride our train through this tunnel, to sit with us in conversation by reading *Mental Health Meltdown: illuminating the voices of bipolar and other mental illnesses*. These inside looks from those who share their stories anonymously and others who identify themselves anticipate that voicing their wide-ranging life experiences with a mental illness will help you gain understanding about differently wired brains. The *seen* physical and *unseen* brain diseases can blend into a win-win for everyone. Thank you for traveling into our world.

—Paul and Arlene

Chapter 1

Helping Others Hold On to Hope by Bravely Telling Their Stories

When Paul felt compelled in the autumn of 2023 to write our book featuring others' stories, he set up a private Facebook group called The Voices of Bipolar. That was our title at the time. We first focused only on bipolar because that is Paul's diagnosis. Since then, with suggestions from our publisher, we changed our title to *Mental Health Meltdown*. Reading each story submitted, it grew into a collection of varied faiths, ethnicities, and stories from Gen Z to senior citizens and all ages in between, both single and married. Their stories are quite different, yet with common themes of struggles, sorrows, and successes!

"His Diagnosis Set Off an Unexpected Nightmare!"
—Michelle, *38, married, one child*

My husband of fifteen years was diagnosed with bipolar 1 with psychotic features in his mid-thirties. Looking back, we recognize that the symptoms were there. They just grew in severity over the years. Being his high school sweetheart, I watched over the years as his fuse became shorter. His moods were more erratic, his emotions volatile, and his grasp on reality was loosening. There were low moments—sudden exits from jobs and violent behavior that he wouldn't remember afterward. But there were also breaks and pauses of peace, which felt like bliss. Each time, I hoped it wouldn't get bad again and that we would live in that state of peace. I now know that I can attribute that to the cyclical nature of the disease. The night my husband was diagnosed was the worst night of my life. He suffered a psychotic episode and thought he was talking directly to God. His voice did not sound like his own. His eyes were black. He was suicidal and threatening towards our son and me. I am grateful for the response of our mental health police unit and credit them for keeping all three of us alive. As devastating as this event was, I am grateful for it. It lifted the fog I had been living in for so many years. I often liken my husband's progression of symptoms to the "frog in boiling water" analogy. It took a shocking event for us all to realize something was very wrong. As my husband completed an inpatient hospital stay, I had time to reflect.

If you had asked me then if our marriage and family could survive, I would have told you no. But I read everything I could find on bipolar disorder. I came to understand that my lifelong best friend was under the grip of disease, and he was not himself. It gave me hope that the real him could reappear with time. Things did not get better quickly. It took over a year for me to recognize my husband again, to see glimpses of the person that I'd married. But, with medicine, therapy (for us all), regular exercise, and good sleep, we are getting a handle on it. I know now that it's completely possible to live a good life with bipolar. Bipolar is still a factor, but it's becoming less of a main character and more like an occasional guest that we can kick out after a few days. This improvement has happened because of my husband's faithfulness in managing his bipolar. I view him taking his mood stabilizers as a daily gift, a love letter to our family.

It's a blessing to help my husband live the best quality of life that he can. A lot of people with bipolar disorder need someone(s) to be their North Star, to notice as their cycle ebbs and flows. They need someone, or ideally, many someone(s), to remind them that it's all temporary when things get hard. It's an honor to be that person for someone. As for me, I appreciate and enjoy the good times more. I will never take a peaceful day for granted again! I'm also learning to weather the tough times with grace and let them remind me of this important lesson: "If you don't have your health, you don't have anything."

Raising a White Flag for Everyone
—Jonny McCoy, *WhiteFlag founder*

I was desperately looking for help. I needed someone to tell me that they were broken like me. Were there others in this much pain? Are our thoughts and nightmares similar? Am I alone? Should I have already taken my life? With paranoia, hallucinations, crippling anxiety, uncontrollable emotions like rage, anger, sadness, and fear, how much longer could I make it on my own? Sure, I had friends, family, and a therapist. But where were the other people who could relate to me? I searched everywhere. That is how the WhiteFlag app was born: peer-to-peer, instant help. Even when planning WhiteFlag, after not sleeping for four nights, I attempted to end my pain. I just wanted to go to sleep—forever was fine with me. But I woke up and enrolled in an executive trauma treatment facility.

Recently married to the love of my life, I used every bit of our money on a fighting chance that I could recover and somehow survive. After thirty-four days of excruciating pain and withdrawals, I emerged from the facility free from Xanax and alcohol and armed with a vision of what I needed to heal. Peer support was a huge part of it. Finally, in 2019, in my home state of South Carolina, I created the area's first PTSD, anxiety, and depression support group. Our online following grew to over one thousand people.

Then, COVID-19 hit. Everyone's mental health took a turn for the worse. We couldn't meet in person, so I had to do something! I started matching people based on their mental health issues and backgrounds. I matched two mothers whose sons had committed suicide. When I saw them post photos together on social media smiling, I knew there was something to it. It's amazing how that event propelled me to create WhiteFlag, not just for me but for others. The short description: WhiteFlag is an anonymous and free mental health app designed to connect people who are suffering to real peers who have experienced similar things.

Like stories of so many challenged by mental illnesses, my story is a long one and still is, with physical and mental pain and successes all mingled together. I'll try to keep this short. In my childhood, I lived in an abusive drama in a family line that included alcohol and suicide. It included a violent dad who favored a belt against my mom and me. A family where we did not talk. A mom driven to alcohol. High school was rough; anxiety was constant and unrelenting. I felt like a nobody. I somehow made it into college, then law school, and became a well-known attorney. My story includes an unjustified arrest, being thrown in jail, and witnessing a guy's suicide right next to my jail cell. I was finally exonerated but scarred and traumatized to the max.

Doing something positive with my pain is part of my recovery every day. WhiteFlag is using what we have gone through and what we've experienced for good—mine and others. Am I still beset with my PTSD, anxiety, and the list of my other mental health issues? Yes, but managing any mental illness by connecting with others is my act of hope!

A Shocking Car Crash Resulting in a Traumatic Brain Injury (TBI) and an Unexpected Ministry

—Dawn Corbelli

I am fifty-five years old, married for thirty-five years, and diagnosed with bipolar 2 disorder at twenty-five years old. Over the years, I have fallen into deep depression, suicidal tendencies, and weeks in bed, not able to function. When one person has a mental illness, the whole family is affected. I was fortunate to have the support of my husband and both our daughters, so I have never been hospitalized. For that, I feel very blessed. My husband says if I take my meds and fall apart, he will always stay. If I purposely don't take my meds and I fall apart, he will leave. He also observes that the difference between me and many other mentally ill people is that I always do what I can to be well. I take my meds like clockwork. That is the key to my wellness, and I live a beautiful life.

My bipolar 2, however, became bipolar 1 after the terrible crash my daughter and I suffered. At age fifteen, Veronica was driving with a learner's permit. Pulling out from a stop sign at five mph, a 4x4 truck going 60 mph t-boned us. Veronica sustained a severe traumatic brain injury (TBI), and I, in the passenger seat, had a moderate TBI, six breaks in my pelvis, and nine staples in my head. Veronica's injuries included a sheared brain stem, which few live from, a severely bruised frontal lobe, eight breaks in her pelvis, two broken hips, a broken left ankle, and a paralyzed left side. All we could do was pray that she would live. In a coma and on life support for two weeks, Veronica spent three months in the hospital. When she awoke from her coma, doctors advised us that Veronica would likely remain in a vegetative state and recommended a nursing home for her. We wouldn't hear of it and prayed for her healing to continue. We leaned on the Lord as we grieved about how her future dreams were crushed. God carried us when we could not carry ourselves!

Veronica had to learn everything over again like a small baby, including rolling over, walking, talking, eating, writing, everything. Today, she still has cognitive deficits, cannot drive or work, and lives at home. We, her parents, have guardianship of her due to her impulsivity and poor decision-making skills that can put her in danger. But Veronica is a happy, loving, empathetic, highly functioning person. Veronica is a miracle if ever there was one. One frequent problem that occurs in a brain injury is mood lability. Veronica has been diagnosed with bipolar 2 disorder.

Together, Veronica and I serve as brain injury awareness advocates. We've taught over 1,050 students, teachers, and counselors about TBI in the past three years, helping others realize what life with a brain injury entails and helping other brain injury survivors, caregivers, family, and friends as well. We are transparent about having a combined bipolar disorder and brain injury. I do not consider these to be a private matter or shy away from talking about it because I want others to understand that having bipolar is not a reason to be ashamed.

Dawn's weekly blog is at her "RAW and REAL" brain injury website (www.dawncorbelli.com). Their book is *Miracle a Day, One Day at a Time: Hope after Traumatic Brain Injury*.

Bipolar Is a "No Casserole" Illness

—Diane C. McDaniel, author, *The Journals from a Broken Mind* (shared with permission)

I had a serious suicide attempt at fifteen and was diagnosed with major depressive disorder. Fourteen years later, I began having my three sons. My moods went wacky after the birth of my third son, and sixteen months later, I was diagnosed with bipolar 1 disorder. Initially, I was angry until it was explained to me that I didn't cause my bipolar. Having a name for my symptoms brought peace to my family and friend support. My friends and family were hopeful that I could be treated with medication and possibly get my life back. I was diagnosed with bipolar disorder the same day that a church member was diagnosed with leukemia. His family announced to the church their need for prayer. The church rallied around them ... supporting them through prayer and with meals. I was encouraged not to go public with my diagnosis. My family suffered in silence because of the stigma in the church regarding mental illness. Bipolar is a "no casserole" illness.

An Abuse Survivor's Good Ending

—Anonymous, *female, 33 years old*

Willpower, perseverance, hope, and determination are what kept me alive. From a young age, trauma was part of my life, whether sexual, physical, mental, or family. I was medicated starting at about ten due to PTSD. By the time I was in fifth grade, I started drinking straight liquor or anything I could get ahold of. The sexual abuse started around seven years old.

By thirteen, I was severely depressed, angry at everyone, and numb inside. I realized I was headed towards two different paths: path one, I was going to become a serial animal killer (I was already hurting animals), or path two, become a prison executioner or mortician. These realizations came at just twelve years old. My numbness resulted in a strong hate for females. I fantasized about killing them. These thoughts were shocking. I decided to opt for the path of being a mortician as a job and maybe the hope of a normal life one day. This was just enough motivation to help me wake up daily and attempt my shot at life.

At thirteen and a half, I was raped by a boy my age. His friends were in on it and kept me from getting away. They physically beat me as well. PTSD was in full bloom at this point. I was evaluated yearly in school due to learning delays. Although my dad was kind and generous, he dealt with serious depression. This led to trauma at home. My parents knew I was in bad shape, and I went to a psychiatrist often. I never told her what was really happening. I had great parents, but I did not tell them about my traumas either.

Before high school graduation, I attempted to kill myself by hanging. When I kicked the stool over, I hung for a moment before the ceiling fan broke. I recognized it as a sign that I was still here for a reason. I could not hide this from my parents. They called my psychiatrist and the police, and I was placed on suicide watch. I had no self-respect, I abused alcohol and drugs, had PTSD and depression, and was groomed by a sexual predator, raped multiple times. Numb inside, I had 0.1 percent willpower to see the light at the end of the tunnel. When I was nineteen, I finally told my parents about all the abuse, my drinking, and drugs, and asked them to put me in rehab; that was the beginning of my recovery. For years after rehab, I went to a psychiatrist weekly, which really helped. I was on meds for my serious depression and

PTSD. My parents have been through so much with me, stood by me, and were totally brokenhearted for me. I love them so much.

Fast forward to today, I am thirteen-plus years sober, happily married, and have an amazing high-level job. PTSD/depression is nonexistent; I am off all medication and no longer need therapy. I have learned a lot on the way, but now I know that my life has been restored, and I am free from the chains of darkness. Hope is a powerful thing! Keep restoring your life daily! Keep getting back up! It's an upward battle but so much sweeter on the other side.

A Parent's Disclosure Causes a Breach
—Angelica

I no longer go to church, but when I did, I went with my family. I never shared about myself because I was embarrassed. My mother had a different plan—she loved to plaster my mental health issues all over the place. Yes, I got support, but to be honest, I didn't want it, not from them, at least. And to have my mom explain everything *for* me, from her perspective, was humiliating. People constantly tried to "help" me with words from God. I got so annoyed and frustrated. This is one of the many reasons I stopped going to church.

Bipolar Is Not Who You Are
—Mike Lardi, coach for bipolar and founder of *The Bipolar Now Podcast* on Facebook and www.MikeLardi.com

About ten years ago, I was in so much trouble that I didn't know which way was up. I didn't know I had bipolar disorder, what that meant, how to treat it, or even where to look for help.

I just knew everything in my life was not good. I lost the place I was living, quit both of my jobs, and was "couch surfing" in my late twenties. I realized I needed to call somebody because my mind and emotions were flying up and down so fast. I didn't know about bipolar and that my mind was going through rapid cycling or that I was rapidly cycling in and out of bipolar depression and mania or sometimes both at the same time.

I was beyond scared. I always kept my mental health issues privately suffering, bearing it alone, trying to be a man.

This can happen to anyone, man or woman. Unfortunately for me (or looking back, fortunately), my mental state deteriorated so fast that the police picked me up and took me to an emergency room due to a severe manic, psychotic episode of bipolar disorder.

In the hospital, I found out more than I thought I needed to know and experienced extreme trauma. However, my hospital stay resulted in treatment, and those medications are the same ones I still take ten years later. The medications give me a little more of an edge and more stability. It takes a longer time for the bipolar to take over, which gives me time to respond and do healthy, productive things for my mental health.

It's been a game-changer in my life. Sharing my story is really what *Mental Health Meltdown* is all about. I'm honored to be a part of it.

Facing the false stigma isn't something that needs to be cloaked in secrecy and shame. We must build a world where someone like me can spend less time feeling ashamed about mental illness and more time building relationships. No matter where you've been, no matter how far down this disease has taken you, there's always a new day to take a new step forward. I find it rewarding to help people with bipolar disorder figure out how to put their lives back together after their diagnosis.

I encourage you to start that conversation and take that step. Remember, bipolar is not who you are; it's a disorder you have, and you can live life with it very well.

P.S. Mike recommends *Take Care of Your Bipolar Disorder: A 4-Step Plan for You and Your Loved Ones to Manage the Illness and Create Lasting Stability* by Julie A. Fast and John Preston, PsyD.

Encouraged to Hide Her Bipolar Diagnosis—She Did Not!
—Tara Bufton, author and founder of *Talking Bipolar on Facebook*

For about five years, I knew I wanted to be a mental health educator before I actually did something about it. At the time, I first saw a need for it for myself and people living with mental health conditions. I thought of it as being an advocate, not an educator. However, I slowly realized that what I had to offer, with my teaching background and ability to express myself, is better defined as education. For me, something about the term "advocacy" didn't fit. Ironically, I became aware of the need to share my experience of living with a mental health condition when I was encouraged to hide my bipolar diagnosis.

I went along with the sometimes subtle, sometimes clear advice to keep it quiet … and I kept it quiet. But that didn't feel quite right to me. I felt that something was so wrong with me that I wasn't allowed to be open about it. It tapped away at my self-esteem.

Here I am now, talking about mental health loud and clear. I no longer live in the shame that secrecy carried implicitly with it. I hope my openness will carry benefits for others who live with mental health conditions. "Stigma"—that word that is bandied about; stigma is real. I hope we eventually learn to accept and normalize mental health conditions. We have come a long way already.

Visit www.tarabufton.com or Talking Bipolar on Facebook.

She Disappeared for Days, Spent All Our Money, but the Power of a Diagnosis Saved Our Marriage
—Robert, *28 years old*

My wife of five years is the true love of my life—and I've almost lost her a couple of times. Yes, we have normal husband-wife spats and disagreements, but none of them have ever risen to the level of nearly ending our marriage like undiagnosed bipolar did. She disappeared for days with no notice, spent our savings on clothing, more groceries than our refrigerator or pantry could hold, and a new car that I was fortunately able to return. Each of these events occurred following a tirade of out-of-control emotion I couldn't understand. I didn't even recognize her as the person I loved and married.

Fortunately, I have come to know more since a manic episode ended with her being stopped for reckless driving, wildly uncontrollable, and admitted to a hospital for her protection. She was diagnosed with bipolar 1. We later learned that it was on her father's side of the family. I am thankful that she has been placed on lithium, enabling her to have more control and awareness of when these "mood changes" begin. We are reading about bipolar and have attended a bipolar support group where we heard about *Mental Health Meltdown*. We are committed to each other, and we want to be part of helping people understand this disease.

She Discovered Where Her Bipolar Came from and Describes Her Bipolar Flip-Switch
—Taunya Lynn, *57 years old*

I didn't know where my bipolar came from until I finally met my birth father. He shared with me that he had bipolar all his life and did not discover it until he was an adult. That helped me to understand many of the things that I have done: staying up all hours for no reason or going from happy to angry to sad at the flip of a switch. I self-medicated with drugs and alcohol, trying to make myself feel better, yet that led to more issues. I have been married six times! All were great guys, but my bipolar would not let me settle down. I got so angry and upset that I couldn't control it! How I acted also hurt my relationship with my children; if only I could change that! I made an appointment, saw a doctor, and yep, bipolar 2!

I still struggle, but I am getting better, learning how to have a conversation, stay focused, and have a healthy relationship with my husband. It's still rocky sometimes, but he loves and supports me, which helps me to be more aware of bipolar and recognize when I'm about to slide into an episode. Miraculously, having a relationship with my birth father is also wonderful and helps because he shares his struggles with me.

Imagine standing in a room with someone quickly flipping the light switch on and off—that's what bipolar is like without my meds. Although I am a nurse, I hate taking the medications because they make me feel slow or sluggish. But without them, my light switch is constantly flipping. My brain never stops, and it plays tricks with my emotions. I'll be happy in one room, but by the time I get down the hall, I'm suffocating in sadness or anger, and at my worst, I become enraged! It's difficult at best. Stress for a person with bipolar can be devastating. I do not process stress or worry the way a person without bipolar seems to do. Sometimes, I can't breathe, and I feel like I am going to break! My mind cannot stop! Thank goodness my husband helps me remember to take my meds when he sees it coming.

God Has Been My Rock Even through Suicidal Times
—William

I have had depression since my late teens, which was finally diagnosed at age thirty-two, and later diagnosed with bipolar at forty-seven. When I first received my bipolar diagnosis, I was scared. My family, my wife and children, saw me in a new light. They realized that I had a serious mental health illness that contributed to my emotions (often negative) being extreme. Long before any diagnosis, I would hit the sides of my head when frustrated. That continued until I worked with a therapist after my diagnosis. When I have mania, I get lots of energy, but I also get mean.

My primary issue was anxiety. I would get frustrated and strike out at my wife and children. I would work at a job for about eighteen months and then quit because I became overwhelmed by work demands. I eventually got on SSDI because my anxiety was overwhelming. I've been in a psychiatric unit four times over the years. The last time I was in the hospital was about five years ago. It was usually for suicidal ideation. I worked hard in group and individual therapy with DBT, a form of cognitive behavioral therapy. I take many meds to regulate my moods and reduce anxiety. With anxiety as my main issue, in fact, I am very irritable today. My strong faith in God has been my rock through even the suicidal times. In the worst of times, I always knew God was with me. I spend a significant amount of time helping others deal with their bipolar.

If God Can Forgive Me, So Can I ... Eventually
—Anonymous, *female*

I was diagnosed with bipolar, PTSD, OCD, general anxiety disorder, and ADHD in my sixties. It ended with a suicide attempt and an inpatient stay that saved my life. I got the meds and support I needed and feel better than I have in my entire life. I have become self-aware and ask for extra help if necessary. I take anti-psychotic meds, among other things.

Looking back, I know I was sick early in my life. I was described as a "difficult, moody child." I always had problems and I was also sexually abused by my brother and had a hard time describing it as abuse because it was *just* inappropriate touching, not rape. So, I felt it wasn't *really* abuse. I never said a word because I was already "the problem child."

I put this in the back of my mind and, until I was forty-four years old, didn't speak a word of it to another soul. Meanwhile, my illness got progressively worse. I suffered from postpartum depression after my second child was born and I was put on antidepressants. I spent the next twenty-four years on nothing but antidepressants. I never went to a doctor and did not ask for help, though I knew something was seriously wrong. I had to be the perfect, quiet, non-emotional adult. I spent so many years faking it that I didn't even know who I was. I let people bully and abuse me because I learned not to say anything.

I finally broke and spent a year and a half manic and spent every dime we had, then stole to cover up my deeds. What would happen if others knew my dirty secrets? I ended up getting caught, and everything began coming out. My attorney made me see a psychiatrist, where I was diagnosed.

After my hospital stay, I was on probation and paying restitution. I feel that I got off easy and deserved a much harsher sentence. I have immense guilt and cannot forgive myself. I can't believe I wasn't strong enough to ask for help. Every day I think about it all day, wondering if I'll ever forgive myself. I'm so embarrassed by what I did, and that's why my story is anonymous. There are a lot more details in my history that fed my illness, but it wouldn't be easier to forgive myself.

Yes, I have been through a lot. So have many other people, and they didn't turn to illegal activity. So why did I? Am I really a bad person hiding behind an illness? I was always so hard on myself to be perfect. I now know it isn't attainable, so I must learn to live with it and move on. Not getting past it will hurt all the progress I have made. After comments were posted on the Voices of Bipolar Facebook page, I am so thankful that I received such helpful comments. Now I pray a lot, and I know if our gracious Father can forgive me, I can forgive myself.

The Dream of a Bipolar Simulation
—Dorothy L.

I am Canadian and disabled. I am a thirty-six-year-old single mother of two. Thank you for the opportunity to be part of the future and help those with bipolar to realize that we are not alone.

My story begins as a child. My parents couldn't handle me due to my outbursts. I hit things and was destructive. I always suspected I had something but never understood it until my diagnosis a year and a half ago. I went into psychosis and was hospitalized. After this hospital stay, I went into a deep depression, with nonstop anxiety attacks and vomiting, which often repeats to this day. It was confirmed. I had bipolar.

Previously, I was diagnosed with generalized anxiety disorder and on meds. My mother stepped up and came to my home to help take care of my kids while I was sick and testing out several different medications. The med testing made me feel even worse. I just wanted it to end—dosing up, then dosing down. It was non-stop until I finally took lithium for bipolar, and it brought me out of depression quickly. I was happy to get a diagnosis. I have been legally disabled since 2011, but most of my family never took my disability seriously until my hospitalization. The trauma of being locked up in a hospital was not at all good. I always wanted to have a good job, drive, and be "normal." It's difficult for me since I earned a university degree, which I wasted by never working.

I'd like people to stop telling me what I should do. "You should get a job." "You should be driving." "You should make friends." These "should dos" are what trigger me. I'm educated, and I know what I should be doing. I just can't. Meds make me tired, needing a nap each day and lots of coffee. I forget words and drop things easily. I cannot drive safely, so I don't. I am too nervous.

Bipolar for me has no good reality, but it's currently controlled well. I have not had depression since I started lithium. I wish there were a simulation for others to feel what we feel, but that's a dream. I'm legally disabled, and no one takes it seriously because no one can see the disability.

Thank you again for allowing me to share my story to help others who feel alone.

We Are All around You
—Sawyer, female, 29 years old

What I'm about to share, some people might consider over-sharing. Others might consider this too personal, and they're right. It is personal, but I'm not alone. There are millions of other stories just like mine. In fact, one in forty adults in the United States have the illness I have. The stigma around bipolar is real, and honestly, I'm terrified to share my diagnosis. I am fearful of the ways this will impact my future and my career. However, if we don't talk about this, nothing will change, and we deserve change.

My name is Sawyer; I'm working my dream job in Atlanta, Georgia, and I have bipolar disorder. The stigma around mental illness caused me to wait to ask for help. By the time I realized how sick I was, I was already suicidal. My best friend found me eight hours before I was going to take my life.

Stigma can be life-threatening; it can stop people from asking for help when they need it. The thing is, people with bipolar have always been around you. We are your coworkers; we are your kids' favorite football coach; we are your kids' favorite teacher. Yet, most of us will never speak out about our diagnosis because of the repercussions. I want my story to be the continuation of a conversation about mental illness, mental health, and stigma. Let's do better. We deserve better.

How a Proper Diagnosis Would Have Changed My Life
—Tammy, 37 years old

I was diagnosed with bipolar 2 in February 2003. My biological father and my half-sister had it. In my early adulthood, doctors told me that I just had depression.

I tried to commit suicide three times in January, and after the second attempt, the hospital took it upon themselves to have me committed to the first mental hospital I'd ever been in. But again, they just treated me for the depression. I stayed for almost two weeks. Then, I was discharged to my husband's care.

About a week and a half later, I tried to commit suicide again. So, back to the mental hospital. The doctors for three weeks observed me. That's when they told me that I had bipolar 2.

At first, I didn't believe it, but after I left the hospital, I had an episode, which was a huge eye-opener for me. If I had been accurately diagnosed with bipolar 2 earlier, my life would have been dramatically different.

Thank you so much for letting me share this with your readers. Hopefully, this helps someone else understand how very important mental health issues really are.

Bipolar People See the World Differently
—Tasha K., *36 years old*

I was diagnosed at nineteen when I ended up in hospital during my first manic episode. Bipolar has impacted every aspect of my life. It has given me heightened experiences my peers could never imagine but I would throw them all away to rid myself of the depth of its utter agony and despair. Converting to Islam and motherhood has proven to be more useful in keeping me alive than any medication, although lithium is essential. Despite this, during the darkness, this illness makes me resent these blessings. Bipolar is a tiring beast. Just ask my husband. But then again, I wouldn't have met him if I didn't have bipolar!

A quick chat on my mother's computer in 2008 saw me develop quite a liking for her online Arabic teacher. One month later, I flew alone to the Middle East and married him. I had no money and no plans. Bipolar was in charge. There have been many challenges. But now, married for thirteen years with three beautiful children, I can say thank you to bipolar for something.

I genuinely believe that bipolar people see the world differently. Our moods allow us to see everything from alternative perspectives within short spaces of time, which gives us a unique understanding of the world around us. This fosters creativity, good conversation, and, unfortunately, at times, pessimism.

Medication for me these days is essential. I did go a few years without it whilst pregnant, and I was extremely unwell. I regret not taking my medication for fear of harming the baby because I believe being unwell mentally harmed the family much more. I've tried so many medications. Some have worked for a while, and some haven't. Some have made me worse.

Now, I am reasonably stable, although I am fighting low moods on various meds. I really have no other option left in terms of medication. I am learning to become more self-aware of my moods as I get older, but my moods are more severe. All I can do is prepare to weather the next storm. May all those with bipolar find the strength to carry on triumphantly! And may those who don't have bipolar rejoice and try to understand what we go through.

I Am GEN Z; It All Started When I Was a Child
—Zackk Biel

In my mind, my story starts at eighteen years old. There was one big hint that I had this disorder, and it was the severe, lifelong anxiety I exhibited first as a baby. I couldn't be taken to new places that often, or else I would get sick. It led to me having a colonoscopy at age ten to try and diagnose my stomach issues at the time. In later years, I couldn't even hold a job without vomiting or breaking into tears. I was prescribed Zoloft and was told it could take four to six weeks to kick in fully. Hearing this, I knew I couldn't make it that long at work. So, I drove to the office and quit immediately after my appointment. While being walked out by my manager, he leveled with me and said he experienced similar events when he was younger and that I could come back anytime. I left, crying on my way to my car.

In the weeks that followed, I sank into a depression of which I was unaware. I went to the ER after a week of no sleep and, on the advice of my doctor, hoped to be admitted. Instead, they said I was having an anxiety attack, gave me a shot of Ativan, and sent me back home. I slept for nine hours that night and woke up in a much-recovered state. Once I had my psychiatry appointment, I was myself, but my doctor didn't know what to do with me. He pushed my symptoms away as being adjustment disorder, but by this point, I was convinced I was dealing with bipolar 2.

Months followed, and I slowly did better and began another IT job in my area. This time, anxiety was not an issue. What *was* an issue was my new depression. A few months in, I'd find myself crying at work and worked from home due to it. Eventually, it built up, and in December 2019, I signed myself into an inpatient facility due to suicidal ideation. It was here that I received my official diagnosis of bipolar 2 disorder.

Of course, like all of us with bipolar, there are a myriad of complications, experiences, and stories that I've lived through. I want to share with the readers that I'm encouraged. I have been stable for over two years, am on the right meds, and am managing well these days, living independently and working full time from home.

Not All Diagnoses Are Correct
—Paula, *79 years old*

I live in Atlanta, Georgia. In 2023, once again, I am struggling with nightmares, anxiety, and panic attacks. Plus, I live with fibromyalgia and chronic fatigue syndrome, which came about in my seventies. I've dealt with mental health issues since I was eighteen years old, all the way from my hometown to Memphis to St. Louis to Little Rock and now Atlanta. Doctors in every city prescribed medication and in St. Louis, outpatient care. The diagnosis was bipolar, except for one psychiatrist who diagnosed me with major depressive disorder and PTSD. *That* I thought might be possible. I am now with a psychiatrist who is excellent and, after many conversations and many visits, said I do not have bipolar. I'm still struggling to understand it all, but I am thankful to have that confirmed. Mental illness in any form is so difficult. Without my strong faith in the Lord, I would not have survived.

The One Decision That Changed It All
—Susan, *59 years old*

I lost my last job when I finally found out I was bipolar. Although I had been in bipolar group classes for years, we all thought I was just severely depressed.

I was also addicted to gambling. I live in Alabama, and for years, I took gambling trips to big casinos in Mississippi. The trips became more frequent and more expensive, and that is part of why I lost my job. My illness developed slowly over the years. Professionally, I worked at a major network affiliate in the master control department, overseeing broadcasting for our station twenty-four hours a day, seven days a week. Detail was everything in that position, and I was an expert, but this illness is ruthless. I began wanting to stay in bed and not go to work.

Then, suicidal attempts led to three hospital stays. During my last two years at work, my suicide attempts were very serious. On my job for ten years, I began to doubt myself. I suffered the shame of missing work, poor job performance, and even not caring about my appearance. I changed when I lost confidence in my ability to do my job, which I was so good at. Everything changed with one decision I made.

All I needed to do was turn left to go to work, but I turned right and headed straight toward Las Vegas. I turned off my phone and drove to Mississippi, where I'd been going for years, and wrote seven thousand dollars of bad checks. I slept in my car, then drove to Las Vegas, Nevada.

I remember stopping at a big truck stop one night and sleeping a few hours, but that's it. During that time, I finally realized I was bipolar. I didn't even gamble for the whole week in Vegas. I just took advantage of the free hotel perks. I seriously thought about driving to Canada or Mexico but realized I did not have a passport. I finally turned my phone on and called my desperate mother, telling her where I was. When I got home, I learned that, of course, I had lost my job. My employer wrote a letter to me that my mother never let me read. When I called a friend at the TV station, he said the staff was told not to speak to me.

My life was a slow descent into a major crash and burn. I even thought of robbing a bank so my family would have more money when I committed suicide leading up to the huge mania episode. I was sick. When the later stages of bipolar hit me, I couldn't work again. I couldn't remember well enough to work almost any job. My application for disability went through on my first submission.

She Said Her Bipolar Was Not an Issue, but It Is
—Sam

My wife has bipolar. When we first met, she said it wasn't an issue. She didn't medicate but had it under control with cannabis. That seemed okay at the time. Now, five years later and four years into marriage, her bipolar is very much real, the biggest wedge in the marriage and my focus. There's no downplaying its importance and how much attention she needs. I try to be helpful and focus on helping her control her mood. I struggle with walking on eggshells and tiptoeing through conversations and chores to keep my wife from fluctuating to a bad place.

She needs me to give, and I have nothing left. She needs support and blames me when she's sad. Unfortunately, I get defensive, and my response makes her worse. If I leave to avoid making anything worse, she views it as abandonment. I've been to jail overnight in this marriage, where I've never had any criminal involvement before. I've had horrible, crushing things said to me that I've never heard from anyone else, let alone my favorite person that I chose to marry out of everyone in this world.

I've never been hit, slapped, or punched until our marriage, and never done that to others. She tells me her behavior is my own doing, that I push her to that place. I've left for the past week and am unsure what I'm doing here. I am wondering how to be a better husband or how she is dealing with her bipolar. It feels like we're growing apart as we spend more time apart.

We are young Christians who try our best to stay biblically aligned. However, citing Scripture and church attendance has also become a source of tension. Life between us is a minefield of stress and upset. I'm tired, confused, lost, and disappointed in general. I thought I was competent in so many ways, but I'm learning that I fall short of my duties and responsibilities and fail every day. It's tough.

I joined an online bipolar group to learn how I can best help and serve my wife. The first thing I learned was that I should have become more educated about bipolar from the start rather than simply accepting what my wife told me. I've learned that bipolar is a brain condition that requires medication prescribed by a psychiatrist and ongoing therapy.

I've learned that her actions are considered spousal abuse. I cannot disagree with that.

If our marriage is even possible to be saved, she needs to take whatever steps are necessary, perhaps even an in-hospital period for diagnosis and treatment. Anything is possible with God. If it's God's will, then we should both take whatever steps are necessary together.

He Was Manic the First Three Months of Our Marriage, but He Got Better!

—Mary

I hope sharing these details will be an encouragement to others, especially those just beginning life with bipolar in the picture. My husband was diagnosed with and medicated for bipolar about six months before we met. He has never gone off his meds, which has been the biggest key to the success of our relationship. Looking back, he was manic for the first three months of our relationship. Once we got into a regular sleep schedule and routine, his mania calmed down.

We got engaged after dating for six months and shortly after moved to a different state together. We did not know much about bipolar and did not realize that changes can be a huge trigger. He went through three jobs within a month, the last of which had a rotating schedule. This really did him in. He became very depressed, and his therapist advised him to quit his job. It was hard trusting her and making that jump. We had an exceedingly tough time for the next month with cycling depression and mania. He cried every day and did reckless things like walking on the railing of our third-floor apartment balcony. It was so hard not knowing what to do. I had to take over everything, including chores and bills. It lasted only a month, but it seemed like forever. He got a part-time job and still struggled with depression, especially those hours he was alone, but it was much better.

Fast forward another two years. He switched to a full-time job for a better salary. It was a work-from-home and travel-around-the-city type job. He was terrible at setting his own schedule, could not get into a routine, and fell back into depression and suicidal thoughts. He was hospitalized for suicidal thoughts for two days and given new meds. The meds helped, but he remained depressed. We then moved to a new city where he had better job prospects. This time, we were smarter—we hired movers. He carefully chose a job with regular hours and an office environment. His depression has been so much less, and he is able to work full time.

He still needs his meds switched every six months or so, but we stay on top of it. We do not wait for things to be dire before going to the psychiatrist. We've learned his triggers, and we know how to avoid them. We put his mental health above everything. If he is not doing well and it's Christmas, we cancel our plans to visit his family, as traveling is a trigger. The best thing for me to do is be flexible. I do not have rigid expectations now, as I did in the beginning, so I don't get upset if he cancels plans. We've had a lot of bumps in the road due to bipolar, but we are solid. I think our bipolar-ship will last a lifetime.

We also learned that money doesn't matter as much. It is a lesson to learn, but he got to a place where he could work, and financially, we made it through.

We have now been married for almost ten years, and his bipolar, as well as our relationship, has only gotten better. In 2020, my husband discovered that, in addition to bipolar, he also has ADHD. Taking meds for bipolar and ADHD has made it so he can really succeed in work, as a partner, and now as a father. He has never missed or stopped taking his meds—this is key!

Another big thing that has helped is meditation. He made a New Year's resolution to meditate every day, starting with guided meditations on a podcast app. Now, he does his own and attends a silent meditation retreat every year! It has completely rewired his brain to be calmer and less reactionary and keeps him grounded and regulated. He is holding down a wonderful job with a weird schedule where he is often on call in the evenings (something he could not do five years ago). I attribute his meditation and routine to this.

We also just adopted a teenager! I thought we would never have kids because taking care of him was all I could manage. But he has been able to care for himself for years now, and we do things 50/50 with me around the house and for our daughter. He still occasionally gets manic or depressed; it never goes away completely. But what I love about him the most is that he never gives up and always works on himself.

Depending on God Alone in Her Bipolar
—JMR, *female, 66 years old*

I've been aware that I was somehow "different" since I started school at age five. I spent nearly every day of kindergarten hiding in a play doghouse unless we were sent out for recess. I kept to myself then, too. I started self-harming before I reached my teens, never where it could be seen. By age fourteen, I began raiding my parents' liquor cabinet to bring myself down and interact in a "normal" way. There was no money for college when I graduated, so I began working full time at age seventeen. Let the parties begin! I had access to my sister's ID and began drinking heavily. Along with that came more risk-taking and sexual promiscuity. Half the time, I didn't even know the guy's name.

My first deliberate overdose was at age twenty. I was left alone in a house where I didn't know the street address and woke up after three days in a coma. My legs didn't work, so I dragged myself down the hall, trying to figure out what to do. I pulled the phone to the floor with me. It took me half an hour to figure out what to do with it (I couldn't remember how to dial) and another fifteen minutes to remember my home phone number. My dad found me and carried me to the car and then to the hospital. Doctors there said there was no medical reason for me to be alive since the number of meds in my system was still fatal. (Of course, now I know my heavenly Father saved me. But I wasn't a believer then.) I convinced everyone it was just an accident and was released with the name of a therapist. At age twenty, I was diagnosed with bipolar and given a prescription for meds—which I immediately threw out without filling, deciding the therapist was a quack. Countless suicide attempts followed, some ending in stomach pumping and mandated holds. This time, when they confined me to the psych ward, I stayed.

A month later, I drove to Ohio to visit a friend over Easter. When I left, Wisconsin was snow-covered, and Dayton was eighty degrees. I stayed and found employment at a Christian-owned company (me, who swore like a sailor). Those people loved me even though I was so worldly, inviting me first to bowl with them, then to Bible classes, then to church. I accepted Christ sitting in my car with my supervisor over lunch hour. I cried like a baby.

Satan knew he was missing a wonderful servant (me), so five months after I accepted Christ, I was raped by my then fiancé and conceived a child. I had completely blocked what happened, so I had no idea how I became pregnant. My fiancé first denied anything, then insisted I terminate the pregnancy. I didn't. In early 1985, I gave birth to a beautiful baby boy. Two weeks later, my family came down to move me and my baby back to Wisconsin. Now, I understood it was time to get serious about my mental health. I saw a Christian psychiatrist and was diagnosed (for the third time) with bipolar. I expressed concerns that if this was a matter of record, my child might be taken from me; he reassured me that if I complied with treatment, he would go to court and fight for me.

I've had my ups and downs since, with one suicide attempt since my son was born, and I have used the suicide hotlines a few times. I wasn't always the most "present" parent, but I was a good parent. My son is now a strong Christian man with a wife and four children. In fact, my eldest granddaughter just celebrated her baptism! I am now a caregiver to my mom (I was Dad's, too, until he passed). I volunteer in the community, especially preparing tax returns for senior citizens during the season. I still live alone, which I prefer (well, I do have a cat). God keeps me busy.

The Difference the Right Mental Health Team Makes
—Rhonda Coats

 I was diagnosed with bipolar in 1994. Unlike some people, I was relieved to finally find out what was happening in my mind. I was clean and sober for over a year, and my life was becoming a nightmare. By this time, I was attempting suicide regularly and putting myself in dangerous situations physically, mentally, and emotionally. The beginning of my bipolar life meant hospital stays and court-ordered treatment at a state mental health center. I was overmedicated to the state of being a zombie.

I was in the middle of a long, very messy divorce and had two small children. I began to educate myself as best I could, and after the year of mandated treatment, I discontinued therapy and treatment there. My GP helped me quit some of the medicine and helped me get into a reputable practice with the best psychiatrist in town and some of the best long-term therapists. That was my true beginning. The psychiatrist and therapist worked with me to remove more medicine and find a formula that worked well for me. They also helped me get into a women's peer therapy group. I was taught DBT, CBT, and life skills and techniques. That was sixteen years ago, and today, I still see the same psychiatrist and therapist. My official diagnosis is bipolar 1, rapid cycling with psychosis, borderline personality, complex post-traumatic stress disorder (CPSTD), and anxiety and panic disorders. My life back then was filled with hate and profanity as a Billy bad-ass biker bitch. Through the healing in therapy and the constant care of two ladies, I have become a totally different, independent, respectful, and responsible lady. My children are now grown, and I am a happy grandmother. My life is full of creativity and loyal friends and family. In therapy, I worked to heal the past; now, I live in the present and prepare for the future. I've had losses, made mistakes, and fallen flat on my face. Resilience is the key that keeps me getting up and trying again and again. Never give up! Some days, I barely function, but those good days are awesome.

Hypomania, Creativity, and Happiness amidst Bipolar
—Kraig Casebier, author of *American Barber in Prague*

At thirty-seven, I was diagnosed with bipolar. It hit suddenly, and I felt like my world had ended. I tried to hide it. I didn't want to be a burden, but it was easily seen by those close to me.

Fortunately, I worked with my brother Kerry as a barber, who helped look after me. I don't think I could have written my book if not for faith, family, friends, and my church. Even with twice-weekly sessions with my psychologist, I rarely recalled what was discussed in previous sessions. For some, the first medications prescribed work; for me, it took years. Side effects were extreme and sometimes worse than the condition they were meant to treat. One of the most frightening aspects was believing I had been thinking clearly, then having a true moment of clarity and realizing I hadn't been in my right mind, battered by waves of depression. When I was not at work, I was in bed with depression. Weeks, months, and years passed—a monotonous blur of time and space with occasional bouts of hypomania. Although potentially harmful, hypomania feels awesome—increased energy, creativity, and a positive attitude usually combined with misguided plans, decisions, and grandiose ideas. You feel like you're on top of the world, and nothing can hold you back. You're excited about life, and people are excited for you.

Having a consistent routine and keeping things organized has always eluded me. I get very little quality sleep and have long bouts of insomnia. On rare occasions, I wake up feeling refreshed and like I can accomplish just about anything. But most days, I wake up feeling tired. Insomnia isn't all bad, though. I tend to wake up around 3 a.m. and can lie in bed for two or three hours before I drift back off to sleep. These early morning hours are when I am most creative. The challenge is to then get the creativity from my head into something constructive like a painting or writing or some other creative outlet. Some days and weeks are more productive than others.

People often ask me how I accomplish so many things or have acquired so many different skills. The fact is most of my productivity comes in bursts. Many days, I accomplish very little as I'm too tired, feeling sluggish, and sitting in a daze. At other times, I can hyper-focus, complete my projects, or learn something new. I've learned to say no, pull back on activities when I'm down, and push myself when I can. Awareness is key. It took years for me to find a medicine that works, but just as valuable was the talk therapy.

My depression isn't as severe now. It manifests by draining my energy. To counter this, I try to do something creative. I usually do a small sketch or painting of a subject I'm well-versed in. I keep it small and simple, making it easy to accomplish. This small accomplishment and the satisfaction I get from creating it builds my self-esteem, which, in turn, starts to energize me.

I think it's important to gauge how much energy we have and how to use it wisely. Certain circumstances and/or people can be very stressful or draining. If I feel like it will be too much, I avoid the situation or cancel. At other times, I feel like I can do anything, but I've learned to be careful about how much I take on. Good things can also be stressful. I tend to get excited about new ideas and projects. I must be careful not to take on too many projects simultaneously. The more I take on, the more pressure I feel. Most of the pressure and stress from these projects is self-imposed. I try to control this by compartmentalizing some of the projects and focusing on others.

Being busy and productive are two different things, and this can be exacerbated when I work on tasks that are easier or more fun than the tasks I should be focusing on. At sixty-two, I'm still trying to get my ducks in a row, but there's always one or two that are running off in different directions. Life will never be neat and orderly, but it is an adventure. When times are dark, I know there is light at the end of the tunnel. I also know there are more tunnels to come on the road ahead. Those dark tunnels shape us and make us who we are. It also gives us a greater appreciation of the light; there is always light ahead.

More than a Manic Monday
—Laurie C.

I've had so much happen to me during the years of mania that I don't know where to start. There's physical and emotional abuse from my spouse, a ruptured spleen, cocaine addiction, and alcohol. Then divorce, hypersexuality, and searching for someone who cares for me. I have three children who don't speak to me because of choices I made when I was manic. I went off my medication for years and made the worst possible choices, all of which have consequences. After being stable for about three years, I've learned that I can be happy despite everything. We can't go back, and guilt gets us nowhere. It just ruins our peace.

I started a way to help others by creating a Facebook group called Manic Mondays, the Bipolar Struggle. In this group, I share my past because I believe that others have made some of my same mistakes and live in some of the same guilt I have had. Guilt is poison; it paralyzes and keeps us in shame.

I'm sixty-two now, and I don't hide my past; I share it with anyone. Stigma is a big issue. I have recently found that it can be difficult mentally and physically for people to understand if they can't see it. And being bipolar just adds to the fact that some people don't want to understand or simply can't.

I think it's the "normies" who have a harder time understanding that not all the stigma is true, especially when it comes to bipolar. We add to the stigma by not speaking out for a myriad of reasons. I'm working to change that.

The Key to Bipolar in Marriage: Communication
—Decima J. Clark, *married*

I was diagnosed in 1972 with bipolar 1 and later bipolar 2. My husband and I have been married for fifty-three years, and he's a wonderful man. I now consider myself a bipolar educator due to the knowledge that I have gained over the years. I read people very well and can feel their feelings when we talk. I graduated from therapy with my therapist almost two years ago, am still on some medication, and see my psychiatrist every three to four months. I have mentored groups in the past, and I am very lucky to have done so. I can recommend books to read and I belong to *BP Magazine* and encourage everyone with bipolar to join. It has many articles, and people share some of their problems. Last year, the magazine stopped publishing, but their emails are available. My hobbies are coloring and singing. My coloring has developed into a business that includes portraits. My husband has helped me and encourages me to continue. I also sing and do karaoke.

All of us should have a hobby to fill in our spare time. Living with someone who has bipolar can be hard. My husband and I have our ups and downs with arguments. My bipolar rage sometimes finds me slamming cupboard doors, hollering at my husband, and taking things out on him.

After fifty-three years, he understands; and after I quiet down, we talk about what has upset me and figure out what I can do the next time I am angry. It helps to talk before the cupboard doors get too loud and the shouting begins.

I encourage communication. Let your spouse know you are having anger problems before it goes too far. Bipolar is hard on a marriage, but we can all work through it. I am seventy-three, and my husband is seventy-five. We've worked through some of the hardest years of our lives, and we're still married. Communicating with each other can work for you, too. Talk before the problems start.

Med-Resistant with a Brain Affliction
—Anonymous

I have bipolar 2. I've been in many relationships (the longest was thirty-seven years), but I've never been married. It's difficult to be in a relationship with someone who has bipolar. I spent years in a hellish existence. I went through more than a dozen suicide attempts and risky immoral behavior. It wasn't until I submitted myself to Christ that I was able to accept my diagnosis and able to receive the help I so badly needed. I still experience episodes, but I am not alone. God walks with me. Sometimes, I look back and rejoice in what God has walked through with me. I was first diagnosed with manic depression around 1976 after I attempted suicide at age twenty. I rejected that diagnosis three times over the years. This was followed by years of seeking the right cocktail medication mix as I am med-resistant.

I only shared my diagnosis with my closest friends. Half of my family denies that I have bipolar, even to this day. I survived being raped in my twenties and chose to raise the child as a single parent with God as my co-parent. It's good for me to remember how Christ has stood with me over the years. However, I am mainly sharing all of this with you because I, too, want you to understand that we are just like anyone else with a physical affliction—ours is a brain affliction.

Injured by a Weapon in the Army and the Painful Impacts on My Family
—Marco Benavides

When I served in the Army years ago, a weapon struck a blow into the back of my head. It resulted in a traumatic brain injury. After I returned to civilian life, I struggled with depression. When going through a depressive episode, I isolated myself from the world. I spent most of my days in bed. I didn't feel like doing anything, and I drowned myself in sorrows and feelings of unworthiness. One day, I received a Veterans Affairs flyer with a message about depression and mental illness. It gave information about making an appointment with a counselor if I was struggling. At the appointment, the counselor diagnosed me with PTSD. I was later also diagnosed with bipolar disorder. Coming to terms with my condition and the subsequent healing process was akin to walking through a dense fog, where every step forward was an act of faith, a testament to the belief that there would be clear skies ahead. It involved a multifaceted approach that went beyond medication and therapy. It was about rebuilding the broken relationships, starting with the most crucial one: my relationship with myself. My struggle with bipolar disorder has been a significant part of my journey, one that has tested me in ways I never imagined. Diagnosed in 2010, my life spiraled into a series of manic episodes, each bringing its own turmoil and challenges. The disorder manifested in extreme ways—the euphoria that felt like invincibility, followed by devastating lows that left me questioning the very essence of my existence. These manic episodes were not just phases of high energy; they were periods marked by reckless decisions, including a spree of irresponsible spending that led me to purchase extravagant items like a Corvette, invest in businesses without due diligence, and engage in other financially draining activities.

My thoughts raced uncontrollably, a whirlwind of ideas and plans that lacked coherence and feasibility. This struggle was not just with the disorder itself but with the guilt that came with it. The manic episodes induced by sleep deprivation and exacerbated by medication turned my world upside down. One particularly memorable manic episode was triggered by a medication meant to treat my depressive state. Instead of alleviating my symptoms, the medication propelled me into a manic state where I became delusional, believing myself to be a supreme being with special powers. This delusion led to a confrontation with the police, an encounter that escalated quickly and resulted in my arrest, a sobering moment that highlighted the severity of my condition.

But perhaps the most painful aspect of my battle with bipolar disorder has been the impact on my family. The erratic behavior and emotional abuse inflicted upon them during my manic episodes have left deep scars, causing them immense pain and suffering. My actions, driven by a disorder I felt powerless to control, have inflicted trauma on those closest to me, particularly my wife and children, who have had to endure the brunt of my unpredictable moods and erratic behavior. The deepest cuts were not the financial losses or even the legal troubles. It was the emotional and psychological toll my condition took on my family. In my worst moments, I became a source of pain and suffering for the people I loved most.

After much counseling, I have not taken any medication in over a year* and rely mostly on prayer meditation to manage the bipolar symptoms. For months now, I have been stable with no manic episodes and God's help with depression. I listen to worship music and attend church daily. It is a great source of comfort and inspiration and gives me new life daily.

Marco's book: *Experiencing God's Love through the Healing Power of the Holy Spirit*

Note to reader: Never stop taking your meds without consultation with your psychiatrist.

I'm a Success Because I'm Me
—Nadia

Five years ago, I was in uncomfortable mania pain, agitation, and super sensitivity. It was not a nice episode; there was no "high." I couldn't leave the house; psychiatric nurses came to support me, and I needed the crisis team's input numerous times. I could barely look after my kids. But my kind, generous, loving husband and mother took over to look after our kids. I couldn't do anything. When I started to get better, the meds made me feel numb, but it was not the sledgehammer it was in the beginning. I gradually built up by going out with my mother and kids until I could deal with my kids by myself. My kids were five and ten years old. I was seriously ill since they were two and a half and seven.

Finally, I felt ready to get a job. I applied at the local hospital, where I'd been a medical secretary for most of my working life. I started small and kept my head down, mostly doing typing and the easy stuff. I really impressed them! I was so pleased to hear that.

I was building a safe little life and working full time. Fast-forward: I became a secretary and then officially applied for my job.

I succeeded! Almost four years have gone by. I now have a new, more demanding job. For two months, I applied to four jobs and got interviews for all four with two offers. The one I really wanted I didn't get, but I did amazingly well even to get an interview.

I won't give up; I am a success. It is because I'm me—because I take my meds, reach out, and accept help.

I Won't Let My Son's Bipolar Keep Me from Him
—Dan Wright

I am a veteran, having served in the US Army for five years and in Vietnam for eighteen months. I survived the Tet Offensive in 1968 and, in 2018, returned to Vietnam for the fiftieth anniversary tour put together by the Twenty-Fifth Infantry Division Association. My first son was born in 1969 and had a normal childhood, yet sadly, his mother and I divorced in 1976. I tried to stay a part of his life and really regret not trying harder to get full custody of him and his brothers.

When my oldest son was in college, he had an episode that was later diagnosed as bipolar disorder. Initially, this condition did not have a negative effect on our relationship. But, one day, when I was at his mother's house when he was visiting, he got really angry with me. We argued, and for fifteen years, we had little contact with each other. Last spring, I called his mother and arranged to see him at her house where he lived. That visit went well, and I saw him again close to his birthday in July 2023.

I tracked down his address for my first visit to his home. He did not invite me in when I showed up, but we talked outside. I have visited two more times and he has not rejected me. I am encouraged that our relationship will get much better. I told him I would try to come over at least once a month and gave him my phone number and address. I made sure to say he was welcome to come to my home any time. I hope he will take me up on this. As a dad, I have learned some tough lessons about myself and my son with bipolar. I am more educated now and hope and pray that we can restore what we have lost over the years. For everyone reading my story, if you are estranged from a family member with a mental illness, do everything you can to restore it before it is too late.

Using My Struggles to Help Others through Theirs
—SSgt Charles L. Peltier

When I enlisted in the USCG in 1980, the world was my oyster. My whole life was ahead of me, and I didn't want to waste a second. Although I did well in my five years, receiving multiple awards and helping others, the boot camp bullying continued into my career and greatly scarred me. The bullying led to chronic migraine headaches and an addiction to prescription narcotics and alcohol—lasting twenty-six years.

After serving in the USCG, I joined a humanitarian hospital ship sailing to many countries for four years. Mercy Ships provide free surgeries in developing nations. I served on the evangelism team. Yet, in 2017, I found myself suicidal—just waiting to die, a candle wick snuffed out. A pastor friend of twenty-plus years came back into my life and helped me want to live again. Eight months of rehab changed my life.

Although I had barely seven months clean and sober, with suicide, depression, and migraine issues still on my record, my pastor asked me if I wanted to visit the chaplain's office and check it out. He recommended me as the wing chaplain of the Air National Guard base nearby, and the base commander approved me. (I had not been suicidal in many months.) I began as a civilian, going to one drill weekend a month. After nine months of serving as a civilian, I re-enlisted in the California State Guard with the understanding that I would serve with the Chaplain Corps. In my four years back in the unit as a chaplain assistant, I received the same E5 pay grade as in the Coast Guard forty years earlier.

I now have six years clean and sober. I help homeless veterans go through the disability process and help men with substance abuse issues, whom I understand from my struggles. When I went into rehab, I was fifty-six years old, and I felt like I had nothing to show for it. I never married and have no children, yet because of Jesus, I am a man of strong but imperfect faith, as are most of us. I gladly serve others.

Holding On to Light
—Wendy M. Weather, *author*

In 1996, just before my twenty-second birthday, I found myself sitting on a bed in a psychiatric hospital with my parents standing over me while a doctor advised me that I had manic depression. I had never heard the term and didn't know what it was, so the doctor handed me a pamphlet that described the symptoms. I scanned through it and then read it more closely. It explained what had happened to me for the last six months. I had known something was not right, but until then, I did not know what. I could not deny that it was the correct diagnosis. Wendy's book: *Holding On to the Light While Living with Bipolar Disorder.*

War Was Becoming a Way of Life for Me
—Anonymous with PTSD

I was deployed to Afghanistan in 2002, came home in 2003, and then deployed to Iraq in 2004. Being a warrior is not a job. It is a noble, honorable profession and a biblical one when done correctly. However, war as a way of life is not what God wants for His people or His soldiers. Sometimes, we were hamstrung about going after their leaders. I saw, in frustration, our soldiers forced to act in the absolute lunacy going on against civilians and the enemy. We went on patrol daily and were often stuck in traffic jams where we always knew we could be ambushed or blown up.

One of the worst moments is seared into my mind in Iraq. I saw the horror after cowardly enemies blew up my buddies with IEDs from Iran. I helped clean out a Humvee where my buddies were murdered. We removed the larger pieces of their remains with our hands and scooped out the smallest pieces with a spoon. When we power-washed the inside of the vehicle, a literal river of blood formed alongside it. I saw "leaders" and psychologists, knowing what soldiers were going through, discharge them from the military, in doing so, tearing them away from their closest friendships formed in combat instead of taking care of those who did the dirty work in following the orders of the command.

Coming home, I could not deal with life. Diagnosed with PTSD, I was in deep pain and escaped into drinking and promiscuity, using a sinful life to flee from what I saw. I only got worse, slowly, and almost imperceptibly, just like the enemy of our souls designs it.

My parents could not help me, nor could my friends. A few years prior to my deployments, I was admitted to a Christian college. After returning home, I inquired if a spot was still open. It was, and I drove there and turned back around the first time. A few days later, I realized I did not have much of a choice in life and drove back to school. It was my last stop. I knew that if I did not go where God and a healthy environment were prized, I would end up in the gutter and possibly dead. God provided me with solid friends who allowed me to unwind my war experiences and provided counselors where I could share my emotions.

In my first semester, I met the wonderful woman who later became my wife. College was difficult, and at times, I almost quit, yet we were engaged in my last semester. She is my tower of strength. This may sound like the perfect ending. It is not. Even when I returned to my faith, in my struggles with PTSD, I have ups and downs, some of them much bigger than others. Whenever I am in a traffic jam, I am triggered remembering the traffic jams from Iraq.

Marriage, fatherhood, and testy bosses are not always easy, but the perfect ending comes in heaven. Returning home to Jesus helped me with my PTSD. From there, my new life truly began. I am still active in the military in administrative positions. While the passage of time has helped, along with other blessings that can sometimes fail, I had to meet Jesus first, the One who never fails. I also must daily choose life over death. Thankfully, Jesus welcomed me home, PTSD and all, despite my sins. He still does for me and others.

Comforting Others with Comfort I Have Received
—Paul Samuels, *author*

I have researched many resources about why bipolar happens and often wonder if three severe wounds to my head as a young boy were the culprit for my bipolar. Looking back, my life seems miraculous. I attribute much to the creative aspect of bipolar and God's blessings. Years before my bipolar diagnosis at fifty-five, I knew something was seriously wrong with me. After Arlene and I married, I willingly got coun-seling many times, asking God to help me change my life. In the early 1990s, I took a frightening plunge to face the pain of my past in a big way by checking myself into a treatment center in Dallas, Texas, for a month. When the therapy began, I dug into my past and, one night, crawled into a fetal position in the corner of my room and cried in agony. One of the nurses knocked and entered, asking, "Paul, are you okay?"

I said, "I just can't stop crying. I'm traumatized about the childhood abuse that happened to me and how I live in shame because of it." His answer was helpful: "Paul, I know it's rough, but believe me, what you have done is so courageous; keep at it. God will let you know when to stop."

I did finally stop and God wasted no time showing me the root of my problems. Years of buried anger over my childhood rejection was quickly revealed. My roots of rejection in physical abuse from my father, sexual assaults outside in my neighbor-hood, and the need for approval ran all through and around my anger. I cried and hurt daily. I learned that I could hurt without having to fix it. That whatever we use to fix our pain will become an addiction. I allowed God to comfort me and enable me to forgive the abuse, just as He forgave all the pain unfairly heaped upon Him. He showed me the depth of Arlene's forgiveness to-ward me. I was and am always astonished by her love.

After a month in the hospital, I honestly thought I would be a normal person (if there is such a thing). However, I was not diag-nosed with bipolar. It was the early 1990s and not as well under-stood then as it is now. I still struggled, knowing something was still wrong with me but not knowing that mental illness was my reality. I was proud of facing my past, but my serious problems with recklessness and self-destruction in promiscuous episodes were part of my later diagnosis of bipolar disorder.

I relapsed into depressions I could not control, seeming unable to stop myself from making destructive choices. It was devastating to me and to Arlene, and I was so ashamed of the hurt I caused her. In the past, I often considered suicide and began imagining ways to end it all. I tried it once, yet a friend miraculously rescued me. I decided I could not commit suicide and abandon my family. Even in my pain and shame, I knew it would deeply hurt them. That thought kept me alive.

After retiring from the mission field and returning home, I learned how deceptive mental illness can be. Yet, God was faithful to me, Arlene, and our family. Even when I was arrested in a manic episode and spent the night in jail, the next morning God used the judge to order me to a psychiatric evaluation. Had the judge not ordered me to have a psychiatric evaluation, I can only wonder what would have happened. The psychiatrist diagnosed me in 2000 with bipolar 2, after years of counseling and a month-long hospitalization behind me. What a joy it was to learn the actual reason for my episodes of wrong behavior, thoughts, and feelings. Throughout our marriage, before my diagnosis, my wife often said that she had never known anyone so desperate to get well. Her love and God's love led to my diagnosis and medication.

My bipolar medication gives me the ability to manage my moods, whether manic or depression, to control my reactions and make decisions to renounce reckless and self-destructive behaviors. The moods still come, of course, but I am more aware at their beginning, which helps me control my reactions more successfully. My moods still overtake me, and I go on overload. One strategy I developed that helps me is to have a *mirror* conversation to confront myself. It is difficult, but it works well for me. Taking naps helps, too; however, the meds have provided stability and helped me to make healthy choices. I wrote this prose poem years ago and found it helpful for me and others.

What Is Bipolar?

Bipolar is a yoyo of emotions: a scream that has no end, a thrill flying higher than a kite, or a fall into the depths of feelings and behaviors I could not control. When I was down, there was no bottom. When I was up, there was no limit. The merry-go-round of bipolar was, for me, both self-destructive and reckless, with no golden ticket to grab. Often, in the downside feelings, I didn't even have the presence of mind to know where the feelings originated. I call these feelings the *"UGH."* In the past, I chose destructive behavior to silence the UGH. I finally learned that whatever I used to "fix" the UGH grew into an addiction. By the grace of God, medication makes my bipolar life better. The meds don't necessarily take away the UGH. However, for me, "better" means the ability to choose positive responses, and remembering bipolar is a mental illness that happens to me. It is not who I am.

Chapter 2
Three Detailed Case Histories

Kathie Maier Rodkey, one of Paul's mentors for *Mental Health Meltdown*, makes a clear, crucial statement about mental illnesses: "There is no such thing as an average mental disease. One of the sad things about mental diseases is that even though people are diagnosed, it does not mean that each one will have the exact same symptoms as someone else diagnosed with the same disease. One chemical change or fluctuation in the brain variances, in their blood work, and reactions to medications and unending numbers of differences in the brain and their anatomy can produce different variations in their behavior."

We are including three of Ms. Rodkey's case studies because they offer added perspectives. The countless details in each case study take readers more deeply into the mental health progressions and challenges each case reflects.

CASE 1

A twenty-three-year-old has been dealing with bipolar since he was fourteen. He inherited bipolar from both the maternal and paternal sides of his family, a very serious double-edged sword. He also suffers from severe anxiety, yet was doing extremely well in school and with sports until he wasn't. The depressive part of bipolar became debilitating. The manic part was easier to deal with, but the added anxiety was disabling. Still, he managed to graduate a half year early from high school, entered an Ivy League college a half year early, and immediately began playing on a varsity team.

Quickly, his life fell apart to the point where he could no longer participate in sports and had to drop out of college and the sport he loved and for which he had received a scholarship.

His parents tried everything to help him: psychiatrists, psychologists, medication, and rehabilitation, but his struggles continued. He attempted suicide three times and was saved all three times with quick intervention by his parents and the police. He has lost control in many circumstances, destroying people's possessions and badly scaring them. Luckily, no one has pressed charges against him.

No medication thus far has helped him cope with bipolar and anxiety. However, he has not suffered a major breakdown in several months. He has received the best SPECT brain scans, which showed brain damage. Playing sports, he was injured, including concussions and an orbital eye injury, among other injuries. He had the colloquially called "Tommy John" surgery to reduce pain and restore stability and range of motion in the elbow when he was only seventeen.

He is waiting for another drug approval, cannot work, and is still depressed and anxious but holding on. He is afraid he will lose control at any time and has thoughts of hurting other people, and that scares him. He has not been taking medications regularly because he doesn't like the feeling of being on pills, especially when they are not helping him. His bipolar voice is unemotional and vacant of personality because of a new medication, but he shared more comments for *Mental Health Meltdown*. He feels terrible since his parents had so much hope for his success in life. He believes he may never be healthy unless a miracle happens and they find a drug that helps him. He lives with his parents; they support him, and he tries to help them, but it is nothing compared to what he feels he should be doing. He has some good days but mostly struggles daily. He knows it is very stressful for his parents, has been in rehab several times, and he believes his family is relieved when he is out of the house.

He has no control over his brain when he goes into manic or depressive mode because it paralyzes him and makes him think about suicide. He hopes the quiet time he has enjoyed for a few months will continue.

CASE 2

This female researched everything possible about her bipolar disorder. She was one of our most informative and wanted to dispel the stigma of mental disease with honesty and openness about her experiences. Aware of the differences between bipolar disorder 1 and 2, she understood that bipolar 1 is a manic episode that would most likely result in hospitalization yet might not have depressive episodes, while bipolar 2 would have depression issues. She exhibited every known symptom of bipolar with severe mood swings from high (manic) to low (depressive) lasting for days, weeks, or months, and mania episodes that involved hospitalizations.

She was diagnosed with bipolar 1 with severe mania but also suffered depressive episodes. The manic episodes presented with irritability, sleeplessness, recklessness, feeling too confident, and racing and confusing thoughts. The depressive episodes caused tiredness and a lack of interest in anything. She often suffered from a mix of both mania and depression at the same time. During severe episodes, she hallucinated and required hospitalization. One of the most critical concerns for people with bipolar is not staying on their medication. There is even a name for it: "anosognosia," which means lack of insight.

In this case, when she started to feel better, she stopped taking the medications, believing she wasn't sick anymore. She didn't realize her brain was playing tricks on her. Anosognosia is the reason why bipolar is so difficult to treat, but knowing about what it does helped her to stay on her medications. She revealed that she was on a medication that has been effective for bipolar disorder since the 1950s. She talked about how people with bipolar commit suicide at a rate of one in three and that she had unsuccessfully tried it at least four times. She even knew that the average national rate of suicide is one in thirty people.

She revealed that lithium was the drug that helped her as long as she remained compliant. Lithium is also known as the drug that truly helps with suicide ideation. When she is manic, she makes horrible decisions because of her inability to understand the consequences. When she is depressed, she thinks about suicide. She wants desperately to avoid going through this hell for the rest of her life. Even on her medications, an episode can be triggered by a lack of sleep or death in the family. She admits to living in a nightmare for most of her forty years of life. She predicted she would go to her grave with bipolar. I am grateful and admire her bravery in providing the most detailed account of bipolar, sharing with me the hell she has experienced. Some of the situations during her manic and depressive periods were life-threatening. While bipolar disorder can put sufferers in danger, all forms of mental diseases can do the same.

CASE 3

This case is unusual because it involves someone who was eventually diagnosed with bipolar 1, with no evidence of any depressive episodes. The severity of manic episodes is the signature of bipolar 1, and most times, it requires hospitalization. As previously mentioned, bipolar 1 may also have depressive episodes, but it is the severity of the mania that defines bipolar 1. Those diagnosed with bipolar 2 will experience depressive episodes.

A daughter's treatment was delayed because the family believed her issues were due to puberty and would resolve. When her symptoms of irritability, poor judgment, risky behavior, lack of sleep, anxiety, and inability to concentrate required hospitalization, she was referred to a psychiatrist. The psychiatrist quickly diagnosed her with bipolar 1 because the mania was chronic with no periods of rest. The doctor also noted there was no evidence of depression. He prescribed the medicine of choice for many decades. The patient was calmer and in control for a while, until she wasn't. She decided when she started feeling good that she didn't require medication and stopped it cold turkey. Anosognosia is common and sometimes deadly for the mentally ill.

Within a brief period, the mania returned with a vengeance, and the patient stole money from her parents and left home. She was now an adult, so her family received limited help. She was out of touch for six months and then returned home pregnant. Her doctor advised that she could not return to the bipolar medication until after the baby was born. Some women use their medications with no repercussions, and others have complications with the baby, especially in the first semester. Others have fewer bipolar symptoms during pregnancy without taking the medication. While she struggled for the rest of her pregnancy, the patient's psychiatrist helped her get through it without the medication, and with the help of her family, she safely delivered her baby. The baby has recently been diagnosed with several health issues not discovered at birth. The baby's mom then admitted to using drugs and alcohol to help with her mania after she stopped taking her prescription.

The patient's bipolar voice was honest and informative. She thought that leaving home would be better for her, yet she didn't realize how delusional she was about her abilities and feelings of grandeur that she could accomplish anything.

She believed without a doubt that she was completely okay after taking the medication prescribed by the psychiatrist and that she didn't need it anymore. She insisted that she hadn't been told that once she felt better, she might perceive herself to be well enough to stop taking the medication. A warning must be included on mental health medications because anosognosia can be a life-threatening situation. The patient admitted she might not believe the warning anyway but said that she met many others with serious mental problems who had stopped taking their medications.

She reported that her mind was always racing with many thoughts, which were exhausting, and that taking her medication helped. When her symptoms began coming back, she became frantic and decided to use drugs and alcohol to make herself feel better. She refused to talk about some of the risks she took while away from home but said she was lucky to be alive. The pregnancy resulted from many sexual encounters to get drugs, alcohol, and other things she needed. She described the risky behavior as exciting at the time, and the thought of doing dangerous things was still uppermost in her mind.

The patient was put back on the prescribed mental health drug immediately after the baby was born and advised not to breastfeed, and again, she complained about not getting that information. All the details were explained but her mind was in such flux that she did not absorb what she was told. Concerns remained about her struggles with the symptoms of mania, and some postpartum issues were complicating it. She needed the medication desperately and was finally convinced of that.

She thought of leaving home because she was concerned that she would hurt the baby. Unlike the last time she left her home, she arranged to stay with a friend and told her family what she planned. She admitted again her lack of comprehension that the medication would take a while to kick in. She was expecting immediate relief. This can be typical, often not understanding medical explanations, which is why it is critical for those with mental illnesses to have good support surrounding them. She was fortunate that the medication did kick in quickly, and she returned home after several weeks.

She knows she will have to take her meds every day. She stopped talking about adoption for her baby. Most importantly, she now understands her mental disease and what she needs to do to keep it at bay. She says her voice will never be silenced again.

—Kathie Maier Rodkey, *A Layperson's Guide to Living with Mental Disease, Free to Be Insane, The Bin of Life, The Customer Isn't Always Right* and *A Grandparent's Guide*

While some of these case studies demonstrate painful and frightening aspects of life with mental illness, we must respond with help and hope wherever we can. With the right kind of support, diagnoses, treatment, and care, we can minimize the impact of mental illness on the individual, their loved ones, and society as a whole.

Decades of studies and research about mental illnesses conducted by physicians, psychiatrists, prison systems, universities, hospitals, and others lack consistency in facts, statistics, agreement, or conclusions. This is often due to the intricacies and complexity of mental illnesses themselves. One fact remains: our country is experiencing what the CDC calls a mental health "catastrophe." By telling our individual stories, we can be part of the solution.

Chapter 3

Celebrities with Mental Illnesses Then and Now

Understanding the contributions and creative sides of mental illnesses, you will read the names of celebrities who have publicly shared that they have a mental illness. Reading their names may help you refute some of the stigmas associated with our differently wired brains. The information will hopefully keep you from saying, "I am out of my mind," when you also read about the "Who's Who" a few centuries ago, not realizing they had a mental illness. Experts today view them as suffering with a mental illness. Gain encouragement as you read that they were some of the most brilliant and successful people, many of whom made wonderful contributions to society. Some, when life became more than they could manage, beloved figures like Ernest Hemingway and Robin Williams took their own lives. (They did not become mass shooters.)

Before diving in, let's look at an interesting article to better understand some of the history of bipolar specifically: "Historical Underpinnings of Bipolar Disorder Diagnostic Criteria."[1]

> Mood is the changing expression of emotion and can be described as a spectrum. The outermost ends of this spectrum highlight two states, the lowest low, melancholia, and the highest high, mania. These mood extremes have been documented repeatedly in human history, being first systematically described

1   Mason, Brittany L., E. Sherwood Brown, and Paul E. Croarkin. "Historical Underpinnings of Bipolar Disorder Diagnostic Criteria." Behavioral Sciences 6, no. 3 (July 15, 2016). https://doi.org/10.3390/bs6030014.

by Hippocrates. Nineteenth-century contemporaries Falret and Baillarger described two forms of an extreme mood disorder, with the validity and accuracy of both debated. Regardless, the concept of cycling mood disease was accepted before the end of the nineteenth century. Kraepelin then described "manic depressive insanity" and presented his description of a full spectrum of mood dysfunction, which could be exhibited through single episodes of mania or depression or a complement of many episodes of each. It was this concept which was incorporated into the first DSM and carried out until DSM-III, in which the description of episodic mood dysfunction was used to build a diagnosis of bipolar disorder.

With that being said, let's see who they are in the present and past. Famous artists, singers, actors, politicians, scientists, and even the Heavy Weight Champion of the World await you!

People Magazine interviewed eighteen celebrities with bipolar disorder. *Rolling Stone* and *The Guardian* are among other publications where celebrities have shared personal details about their bipolar. A Google search of their names provides more insights about their bipolar. A search on TEDx or YouTube under "bipolar" offers a great menu where you can learn more about bipolar than you ever wanted to know! Mental illness does not need to remain a mystery.

Along with the celebrities below, many more ordinary, brave people have a mental illness. They have used pen and paper to pour out their lives so that you may understand how this disease of the mind is nothing to fear simply because its symptoms are not as evident as those with physical illnesses. I am one of them. I understand how difficult it is to talk openly about mental illness, knowing that others may hold on to stigmas.

We appreciate these celebrities who have shared their private medical information and hope that their openness will influence the public's understanding and encourage others with mental illnesses to be unashamed of having bipolar and other mental illnesses.

Simone Biles, the world-famous gymnast, stepped away from the Tokyo Olympics in 2021 due to mental health issues. She has become a great mental health advocate.

Mariah Carey was diagnosed in 2021 but lived in denial and isolation for years.

Carrie Fisher, best known as Princess Leia, was diagnosed at twenty-four.

Bebe Rexha, a singer, said, "I'm bipolar, and I'm not ashamed anymore."

Mel Gibson, in a 2008 documentary, said he has bipolar. Demi Lovato learned she had bipolar in 2010 while in a clinic.

Russell Brand published his autobiography in 2007, where he discusses his experience with bipolar.

Brian Wilson of Beach Boys revealed that his bipolar left him unable to compose for years.

Kurt Cobain of Nirvana, who lived with both ADD and bipolar, committed suicide at twenty-seven.

Jimi Hendrix, a rock star guitar legend, wrote a song called "Manic Depression," chronicling his experience with his mood swings. He died at twenty-seven in 1970.

Ernest Hemingway, a Nobel Prize-winning author, was prone to manic-depressive behavior throughout his life.

Ted Turner, founder of Turner Broadcasting and CNN, has spent much of his life battling bipolar disorder and depression.

Catherine Zeta-Jones battles depression and a diagnosis of bipolar disorder.

Vivien Leigh, most famous as Scarlett O'Hara in *Gone with the Wind*, was diagnosed with what was then known as manic depression.

In this list of famous folks from the past, keep in mind that their mental illnesses did not prevent them from achieving their fame or contributions.

AJ Mendez	Eliot Jonathan Hay	Kay Redfield Jamison
Brooks	Tim Burton	Maurice Bernard
Edgar Allen Poe	Michael Slater	Tom Waits
Ozzy Osbourn	Kanye West	Buzz Aldrin
Drew Carey	Isaac Newton	Tyler Fury
Virginia Wolf	Linda Hamilton	Patty Duke
Vivien Leigh	Agatha Christie	Sophie Anderson
Frank Sinatra	Ludwig Boltzmann	Peter Wentz
Mark Twain	Liz Taylor	Patrick Cornell
Vincent van Gogh	Plato	Richard Dreyfuss
Halsey	Marilyn Monroe	Selena Gomez
Ralph Waldo Emerson	Sinead O'Connor	Robin Williams
John Day	Ludwig van Beethoven	Abraham Lincoln
Jane Pauley	Jean-Claude van Damme	Winston Churchill
Thomas Stearns	Hans Christian Anderson	Stephen Fry

Most of us are everyday folks, not famous and not celebrities. Reading this list of the famous reminds us that mental illness is no respecter of individual persons, people groups, politics, professions, or religions. Mental illness is a universal malady that lands on the doorsteps of multi-millions in our global community to whomever and wherever it wishes.

Our next chapter addresses mental health within the spiritual dimension. Whether or not you have a spiritual practice or are of a different faith than my and Paul's Judeo-Christian faith, we welcome all who are challenged with mental illness to the

conversation of spirituality and mental health. In one way or another, we are all touched by the common practices and belief
systems around us.

Chapter 4

A Church Takes the Lead

While authoring our book, it occurred to us that amid all the enormous, amazing humanitarian ministries churches enact both in the United States and globally, mental illness ministries are not high on the agenda of churches in all denominations. Grace Theological Seminary observed in 2021 that the stigma of mental illness among Christians is somehow elevated above mental illness struggles themselves. https://seminary.grace.edu/mental-health-and-the-church/

Recent history indicates that Christians have simply been encouraged to pray for mental illnesses to go away. However, mental illness exists almost equally inside the walls of the church as outside. The seminary reports that "92 percent of pastors claim their church is equipped to care for mental health crises as traumatic as suicide." Yet only 4 percent of congregants commented that "their pastors were even aware of a loved one struggling with suicidal thoughts." Stephen Grcevich, MD, in *Mental Health and the Church,* observes that the "North American church has struggled to minister effectively with children, teens, and adults with common mental health conditions and their families. Yet, he notes "the absence of a widely accepted model for mental health outreach and inclusion is a challenge."

Now, pastors and their churches are beginning to consider how to offer help to individuals and families in need of support for mental illnesses. We have included a sermon that Dr. Kirk Walters preached in the summer of 2023. We hold it up as a fine example to pass on to your religious groups to begin understanding how to design outreach for our hurting nation. With his permission, we are honored to share Dr. Kirk Walters' teaching at Mt. Paran North in Marietta, Georgia.

> Many people with mental illnesses are struggling in silence. A church where people come with their brokenness, hurt, and shame is a church that cares for those with mental illnesses and their families. Breaking the silence makes room for God's renewing help. Stigmas associated with mental health are prevalent in churches, institutions of higher learning, and our culture. I am here to tackle it upfront by naming three stigmas that we must get beyond, followed by three truths.

> The first stigma is that we sometimes misrepresent what mental illness is by using psychological words in a casual way. For example, "I am so depressed because my team lost." We minimize the reality of what the issue really is. Your team may be the worst team ever, but you do not have depression. Depression is a *clinical* condition where someone is fighting their own biochemistry just to survive.

> When we hijack terms and use them in another way, those with mental illnesses might shrink back or stay in a shell of darkness, looking for a way out. Mental illness is just that—an illness. Yet, stigma is associated with someone who has chemical, biochemistry, or genetic difficulties.

> Stigma number two is the idea that mental illness is only a modern problem that appeared a few years ago. Some say, "Back in my day, we didn't have these issues." Yes, we did. Mental illness has always been a part of the human condition since sin entered the world. Always.

> Some of the heroes in the Bible dealt with difficult mental health problems. Abraham's grandson Jacob,

whose name was changed to Israel, had twelve sons who became Israel's twelve tribes. Jacob suffered from intense family trauma, today called PTSD. He was detached from his family, could not sleep, suffered from angry outbursts, and irrational behavior trying to protect his youngest son, Joseph, to save his family. Yet God used him to establish the nation of Israel.

When an angel came to Gideon, calling him "a mighty man of valor," Gideon was having a panic attack—clinically. Israel's enemies were on the march, and he hid in a wine press, threshing wheat. God gave him clear instructions, which Gideon first avoided, went into isolation, and criticized himself. Yet, when he finally obeyed, God used him to bring victory to Israel.

Israel's first king, Saul, had all the characteristics necessary to be a good king. Yet, today, he could have been diagnosed as having bipolar disorder. His manic highs, racing thoughts, and escalating anger threatened David when Saul threw a spear at him. A major depression episode immediately followed.

I love the authenticity of the Bible. God could have written the Bible saying that the heroes of the faith had it all together, never suffered, and never had problems. But He did not do that. Mental health is not a modern issue. It is a human issue.

Stigma number three occurs when we think the answer is one-dimensional. We are multidimensional beings: spirit, soul, and body. First Thessalonians 5:23 defines it this way: "*May God himself, the God of peace, sanctify you through and through. May your whole spirit, soul and body be kept blameless at the coming of our Lord Jesus Christ.*" As a pastor, it is my responsibility to share the good news with both believers and non-believers. When sin came into the world through Adam and Eve's free choices, sin altered our spirit, soul, and body. We became susceptible to physical diseases. Our souls—emotions and minds—could become subject to mental ability and mental illness instead of functioning the way God originally planned. Sin's entrance creates chaos born out of our wrong choices. Yet, God redeemed our very lives when Jesus paid our sin debt on the cross. After His resurrection and return to heaven as our High Priest, He left us His Holy Spirit of comfort and counsel behind. These eternal gifts are available to *everyone, no matter your past or your struggles.* Repenting and then asking Jesus to live in our lives to guide and reshape us gives us hope.

Through Jesus's sacrificial death on the cross, our dead spirits live again.

Mental illness occurs in specific and complex ways. Using one solution to fix a multidimensional problem does not work. For instance, we take medicine, but we ignore our spirit's need for worship and Scripture. Or we sit down for therapy but don't eat right or exercise. Some only address mental illness through faith, believing that if you pray enough, believe enough, and read enough, you will overcome.

When nothing works, shame sets in because we think we—or God—did something wrong. The stigma of shame, more than any other, is why so many believers suffer in silence. If shame is what you feel today, I want you to know that God loves you so much. You are not doomed. You are not irreversibly damaged. You are loved, adored, and celebrated by our heavenly Father.

Whatever our culture or what someone may have said to you, *it is not* a sin to have a mental illness. Your identity is not based on your illness. Your character is not defined by your brain chemistry, clinical depression, or PTSD.

I also want you to know about victory in Christ. On the cross, it is no accident that Romans forced a crown of thorns on Jesus's head, where the most intense battles take place … in our mind. Because of Jesus, you are going to make it; peace and joy are attainable. No stigma, no symptoms suffered, and no amount of shame can undo what Jesus has already provided for you through His sacrifice on the cross.

Three truths I want you to know—if you or someone in your life struggles with a mental illness, these are valuable.

First, God is present in your struggle. It is tough to believe when you are having a panic attack, a loved one is in a schizophrenic episode, or when you are deeply depressed. God seems nowhere to be found, yet often, we are grabbing onto a false theology that says, "If things are good, God is present," and, "If things are bad, God is not." Wrong theology. In Psalm 139:7–12, David is in a dark depression. In part, the king cries out, *"Where can I go from Your Spirit? Or where can I flee from Your presence?... If I say, 'Surely the darkness will overwhelm me, and the light around me will be night,' even darkness is not dark to You, and the night is as bright as the day."*

According to the Bible, there is no darkness, no therapy session, no hospital room, no day, no second in your suffering or undergoing a challenge where God is not there. However, you ask, *"If* God is present, then why am I still struggling?"

Sometimes, we assume that grace only comes in one form. Grace is God's power doing in us that which we cannot do for ourselves. However, often, the only grace we ask for while undergoing difficulties is *delivering* grace.

After years of study, following Christ, pastoring, and living through firsthand experiences, I have found three kinds of grace that God pours into our lives.

Grace that fixes something *in* you. Grace that fixes something *around* you. Grace that *carries* you through something.

The apostle Paul is a case in point. He wrote more of the New Testament than anyone, planted more churches, had a miracle-working ministry, and yet he suffered from a physical ailment. In 2 Corinthians 12:8–9 (NLT), Paul writes, *"Three different times I begged the Lord to take it away. Each time, He said, 'My grace is all you need. My power works best in weakness.'"* God chose to give Paul a grace that didn't fix him or even make things easier—He gave him a grace that carried him through every single day with his "thorn in the flesh."

If you have prayed, believed, and asked, God has heard you, and He has given you grace. It is not a lesser grace, and it may not be a permanent grace. His grace may help you through this season right now, then He brings you out of it later. Or, like Apostle Paul, God sustains you and does something in and through you, which assures you of His strength even in your weakness. *One or all three graces at separate times helps you get through another day.* The fact that you are still here and stepping forward is proof that God is present and you are receiving His help now. That is the first truth.

The second truth is that God works through miracles *and* medicine. It is humorous hearing opinions from different camps. People who use medicine are painted as if they have given up on God. And people who believe by faith are painted as if they are giving up on science. Both solutions come from the same source. God did miracles in the Bible *and* does them today. Yes, that means He can reset biochemistry, rewire neurology, heal trauma, and neutralize painful memories. He still binds up broken hearts and releases a flood of joy in an instant. We ask, we take steps of faith, believing that God still is in the miracle-working business. At the same time, God also works through medicine. Our indescribable God is one of omniscience, a compound word that means *all-knowing*. Here is truth—if God possesses all knowledge and He has been around longer than anyone in history, that means *all* knowledge comes from Him.

Brilliant medical minds are brilliant because God shared *His* brilliance with them—and sometimes God displays His power through medicines. King Hezekiah, one of the best in Israel's history, suffered some kind of skin lesion and was at the point of death. God sent the prophet Isaiah to him with a prescription. In Isaiah 38:21, Isaiah said to Hezekiah's servants, *"Make an ointment from figs and spread it over the boil, and Hezekiah will recover."*

We now know that in ancient times, the ingredients they used with figs were a common medicinal treatment used to treat skin lesions and infections. God healed Hezekiah in a medicinal way. If you must use medicine, that does not mean you lack faith. Sometimes, God sends healing through the skill of someone else to regain your health. I am always surprised by those who criticize using medicines. It can be selective, for instance, by criticizing taking Prozac but having no problem taking penicillin.

If therapy is helping you, God is helping you. A prescription working for you is God working. It is time that we take these spiritual stigmas away from mental illness. When we stigmatize mental illness, we drive people back into the shadows when God wants to bring them into His light. Healing happens in numerous ways through therapy, prayerful deliverance, and medicine.

Nevertheless, healing comes in a powerful way through relationships. God brings those with mental illness into a loving community where they are accepted and walk alongside them. This is essential.

The third truth is if you have a mental illness, God's calling on your life has not been lost. Accompanied by shame, its powerful force tries to predict a shameful, false future. No matter who you are—a parent, a teen, man, woman, leader, older or younger, your mental illness may be echoing, "My emotions shouldn't be this unpredictable if I am a Christian," or "I should have it more together." Or "I have faced so many failures; will I ever get better? Are there any more answers?" Use the Bible, the words of God, in your battle against shame. Hold shame up against God's promises. Here is one of many promises in Romans 11:29: *"For the gifts and the calling of God are irrevocable for he does not withdraw what he has given, nor does he change his mind about those to whom he gives his grace or to whom he sends his call."*

If you are in Christ and suffer with mental health issues, it does not mean you are less of a Christian. Even in the worst episodes going on in your life, those moments do not undo God's calling on your life. They are irrevocable. In our society, many feel broken. Some of you may not hold to the Christian faith, or you may follow another faith or have no faith. The Bible is wide open to you, too. Because of mental health challenges, you wonder if there is any hope. Understand that we are all broken in some way. One brokenness is not better or worse than any other brokenness. When we place our lives in God's hands, He helps us overcome our shame, adds grace to the broken places, and uses us to walk alongside others in God's wonderful masterpiece.

When I put this message together, I didn't realize how personal it would become. My wife, Laura, battled cancer three times and finally passed away about a year ago. I never met a woman who had the faith she had. When she walked into a room, her smile lifted the room, and her laughter was contagious. Laura had a hotline to Heaven when she prayed for others. You don't know that for the last few years, Laura struggled with crippling anxiety and panic attacks that only I knew. Although she had a doctor and medicine, sometimes she could not leave the house, and we canceled plans or a church event because she could not face anyone.

What I hope you will see in my transparency is this. The woman with the greatest faith I have ever seen struggled mightily at times with a mental health challenge that gripped her. My heart today is that somehow, someway, if you are living in shadows and not telling anyone, walk out of those shadows today. Please tell a friend or a loved one; call the church. We have a Pastoral Care and Counseling Department. Beyond that, if you need clinical help—we will refer you and walk beside you.

Stop allowing the enemy of our souls to imprison you in fear and darkness when God wants to call you out into His marvelous light. Within your struggles, you may find yourself praising God for His help. Walk in the healing and the grace that is available in a community waiting for you in Jesus's name.

Chapter 5

My Life with Paul

Fortitude Together within Mental Illness
—Arlene Bridges Samuels

Paul Leon Samuels is my husband. We have not only co-written our book, but we have co-written each other's lives as a team with commitment, humor, and a life-giving God, the most Divine Editor and Wordsmith in the universe. Our marriage has survived against all odds. I'm sharing my story as *a rope of hope* for anyone walking alongside someone with a mental illness. When we first married, I made a pronouncement: "Paul, if you ever lose your handsome head of hair, I will divorce you." LOL! At eighty years old, Paul still has a great head of beautiful white hair, and we are still together!

> *"The beauty of life is that every day we have another chance."*

These hopeful words, penned by Paul, my "poetry man," took root in my journey with him, planted in seasons of heartaches and happiness. Our marriage is proof for one of my descriptions of God, the Supernatural Specialist of Rescue Missions! What a joy to share my experiences navigating this journey as Paul's wife and partner for life.

Everybody Loves a Parade

Paul and I grew up in totally different worlds: a Jewish guy from the South Bronx and a gentile daughter of the South born in Raleigh, North Carolina, and later growing up in Florence, South Carolina. I enjoyed an unusual childhood since my daddy owned a professional parade float company in the 1940s called UNIVERSAL DECORATORS, among only a handful in the South. My parents—bright, fun-loving, creative, and loved by those who knew them—affirmed my younger sister and me, cheering us on in all our activities. We often traveled as a family throughout the South beginning in the late 1940s before my sister and I entered grammar school, then on holidays and in summer. When I got my driver's license at fourteen, I joined our crew and pulled twenty-five-foot floats over two-lane roads for spring and summer festivals, Christmas parades, and centennial celebrations stretching from Virginia to Alabama.

Riding along in one of their fleet of cars or trucks, Mother, Daddy, sister Jane, and I often sang songs acapella as a quartet. As a child, I learned how to safely drive a straight nail. Stapling fringe, festooning, foil, and floral sheeting on a wooden float frame transformed it into beauty. Featuring swans, a candy house, a little train with a caboose, a Santa Claus float, and other eye-catching designs, my sister and I spent hours jumping from one float to another with our imaginations in overdrive.

One newspaper article described Daddy as an "architect of dreams." Our family enjoyed the patriotic marching bands and the fruits of our labor in our "business of happiness" for thousands of parade-goers. My childhood set the stage for my "eclectic" life, first overflowing with fanciful themes and later multiple contrasting interests and professions that I found fascinating.

An Eclectic Life and Interests

I grew up in a big Southern Baptist church in Florence, South Carolina, where I sang each year in the graded choir and was baptized at seven years old. On a retreat with our outstanding high school youth group, I encountered Jesus in a personal way. At our new country high school, friends and activities were plentiful.

Graduating from Winthrop University in South Carolina, I majored in philosophy and religion and minored in history and sociology. Atop so many floats, Daddy nicknamed me "Miss America." In my sophomore year in college, he beamed with pride when I won the "Miss Florence" title. My multi-talented mother made my beautiful gown and *all* my prom and beauty contest formals. After college, I earned a master's degree in rehabilitation counseling from the University of Alabama. Roll Tide!

After graduate school, my eclectic interests took hold in positions with Head Start, church staffs, Young Life, inner-city schoolteacher, professional folk singer, founder of Southern Onion Singing Telegrams, refugee resettlement director, mission field with Mercy Ships, then Youth With A Mission in Romania.

For almost twenty-five years, I have held positions with Israel Always, the American Israel Public Affairs Committee (AIPAC), and the International Christian Embassy in Jerusalem (ICEJ US). Beginning in 2020, I now write the weekly feature column at The Christian Broadcasting Network Israel.

Unfailing Love

Why am I sharing my list? It is evidence of God's unfailing love and mercy, allowing me to live a fulfilled life. Childless for twelve years, God then greatly blessed us with two infants in adoption miracles, our son at five days old from Charleston, South Carolina, and later our daughter at twenty-eight days old from Romania. We treasure our closeness with them as adults. Despite times of brokenness and pain with Paul's undiagnosed mental illness, we are indeed recipients of multiple rescue missions from God and our friends.

Our journey began on January 24, 1976, when Paul walked into an Atlanta delicatessen for lunch. I worked as a cashier, which allowed me time to prep with added guitar lessons for my folk singing gigs. (I had resigned from my stressful inner-city teaching position.) South met North, Gentile met Jew, and Paul's persistence opened my heart as my lifelong "groupie." With more joys than sorrows, Paul's episodes of undiagnosed bipolar tarnished our marriage, yet my upbringing served as an excellent preparation for what lay ahead.

My Parents' Fortitude Shaped Me for Marriage

In an unusual chain of family events, my handsome daddy was fifty years old when I was born. He and my beautiful mother fell in love in a May-to-December marriage. When Daddy founded his parade float business, it required seasonal travel. Mother stayed home with my younger sister and me. When I was eight years old, Daddy suffered a freak accident while looking at an engine under the hood of one of his business cars. The hood fell on his head, and all seemed well. However, the next morning, he woke up unable to walk *or* talk. The doctor's diagnosis was not hopeful.

He predicted that Daddy would never walk again. In 1954, the high level of physical therapy we enjoy today was not plentiful.

At fifty-eight years old, my entrepreneurial daddy decided to create his own brand of physical therapy. He must have written notes since he was unable to talk. He asked "Heavy," one of his employees, to come each day, lift him out of bed, and carry him into the front yard. Heavy, who could have been an NFL fullback, placed Daddy on an unimpressive but useful plywood walkway with wooden railings.

As an eight-year-old watching this almost daily scene, I witnessed my daddy's determination and Heavy's compassionate help. A year later, Daddy walked with a cane, his speech returned, and when I grew a little older, I pushed him in a wheelchair when he needed it.

Daddy showed me his fortitude, which was aided by God's help through Heavy. He returned to work and joined my once stay-at-home mother, who had shifted into the role of an executive businesswoman. With a disabled husband, two little girls, and a business to keep alive, she quickly stepped into her role as a superb example of loyalty and added her own fortitude to our family story. Mother and Daddy worked together as a team from that time on. Their example, deeply embedded into me as their daughter, gave me the fortitude I needed when Paul and I faced his undiagnosed bipolar, which brought emotional pain for both of us.

One of the Best Days of Our Lives

Finally, at age fifty-five, after years of willing hospitalizations, counseling, and prayers, Paul's diagnosis of bipolar 2 became one of the best days of our lives. The psychiatrist described his two main symptoms. "Your bipolar produces recklessness and self-destruction in your addiction." Those two words flashed like neon lights as answers to our questions about Paul's episodes. Finally, we understood the backdrop for his addiction and that his brain disease fueled acting out, producing shame, guilt, a suicide attempt, and frequent suicidal thoughts.

Early in our marriage, I called my servant-hearted, outgoing, multi-talented husband a "diamond in the rough." However, a diamond's journey is long and hard. I often identified with it. From two hundred feet underground, intense cavernous pressures, and temperatures soaring above two thousand degrees, the carbon atoms eventually transform into crystalline, are then mined, and undergo a meticulous process of polishing, grinding, and cutting. Lastly, the emerging diamonds are boiled in acids to remove dust and oil; eventually, a rough stone becomes a gem. The famous Persian poet, Khalil Gibran, once said, *"Perhaps time's definition of coal is the diamond."* Yes, time. Diagnosed for twenty-five years now at this writing, our coal is a diamond, still with rough edges and not perfect by any means; yet, it is a precious gem, a symbol of mutual hard work and outrageous commitment.

A Promise and a Presence

My fortitude—and why I stayed—remains because of a promise and presence. When Paul and I first met, we had already fallen far away from the Lord for unwise and willful reasons. During my five prodigal years, I developed a drinking problem and lived a worldly lifestyle. A few months after we met, the aspiring poet and the folksinger moved to Hilton Head Island. Despite our love and the idyllic beauty surrounding us, our partying left us empty, and we knew why. We had abandoned our faith before we ever met. We began attending a *Spirit-filled* Episcopal congregation where an assistant rector and his wife invited us to their small house church group. Through them, God brought loving believers into our lives to pray for us and guide us into repentance. We renewed our commitment to Jesus and settled into rebuilding our lives. However, Paul's path of consistent restoration was incremental, taking small and big steps, sometimes failing.

I dare say most marriages face problems, some bigger than others. Often, the feelings of love disappear. Outrageous commitment must kick in when feelings desert us. I drew my commitment from an unusual encounter with the Lord. One night in the late 1970s, lightning struck in a thunderstorm of confession, and not over the nearby ocean where we lived. Paul, mired in his own shame, admitted to another brief sexual encounter. No saint myself, in my rage, I screamed at him and swept everything off our dresser, breaking everything. I then threw my treasured Bible at him. (Paul later had it rebound in red, my favorite color, with my name engraved on it.)

Pulling out my suitcase to pack, suddenly, in a one-of-a-kind moment, the Lord communicated to my mind and heart. Only Jesus's powerful words could have penetrated my rage since I was certainly not having a prayer time. "Arlene, you have My permission to leave. It is unfaithfulness. If you choose to stay, I will give you the kind of husband you always dreamed of, and I Myself will keep you emotionally stable."

This, my friends, is why I stayed. Words, brief yet momentous, became more than enough to sustain me. I chose to stay because I had already lived the empty life of a prodigal for five years. I wanted no part of it again. I knew I would be in the best hands, believing God's specific promises rather than returning to a self-centered life. In the years ahead, I drew strength from that one profound moment. It is wise that the Lord did not tell me that the healing process would take twenty years to complete before the bipolar 2 diagnosis finally came!

Divorce lingered in the back of my mind. I questioned myself, often wondering if I was enabling Paul by staying or how his mental illness would affect our children. We still spent many hours in couples counseling. The Lord has indeed kept His promises for my emotional health by giving me a secure self-image and a good dose of healthy independence. I never blamed myself for Paul's acting out since it predated our marriage, a long-time escape hatch from his painful growing-up years. I was confident that his love for me was deep—no affairs, only brief, occasional acting out.

Paul's desperate desire to change and his decision to enter a month-long therapeutic counseling program gave me hope.

Although he gained ground for healing his emotional pain, he was still undiagnosed. Relief came for seasons without acting out, but we had no clue about the triggers into sinful behavior after all the counseling, prayer, and hospitalization. I did not excuse Paul's choices nor minimize the pain. Yet the chemical imbalance, his painful childhood, sexual abuse, and emotional escape hatch into addiction made sense after his bipolar 2 diagnosis in the context of the two descriptions rendered by a psychiatrist: recklessness and self-destruction.

I have described our marriage in two ways: a "beautiful disaster" and a "tattered quilt" full of vibrant colors, sometimes torn apart yet always lovingly stitched back together by the Lord's hands, and our mutual investment in each other. An immense part of Paul's investment in me was, and is, his heart of service. He literally finds joy in it and shines as a man, always willing to bless me with his lavish acts of service, no matter how small or big. I have kept my picture of Paul as a "diamond in the rough." He wanted to get well more than anyone I knew, a man on a mission to change and willing to go to any lengths. The Lord preserved me and my hope. Although hope sometimes comes with a high price tag, our true treasures are worth waiting for and always cost more. I am glad I stayed!

Actively living out his life verse in 2 Corinthians 1:3–5, to comfort others with the comfort he has received from God, is a rewarding journey for both of us. He generously encourages others. I am indeed proud of him as a co-facilitator for in-person bipolar support groups at our church.

I understand bipolar more clearly after attending his groups as a support person, listening to others' symptoms and stories, and refreshing my past knowledge with updated information. I am better trained now to interact with Paul when he is experiencing bipolar moments, whether depression, racing thoughts, or shame from his past, which still overtake him. Paul graciously receives my observations when I sense the beginnings of a mood change of which he is not yet aware. I understand that bipolar cannot be cured. Although I did not hold a position as a rehabilitation counselor after graduate school in 1970, I am grateful for it.

Does Paul have bad days? Yes. Do I have bad days with impatience and tiredness? Yes. However, his faith, his generously given love for me and our adult children, support from friends and groups, educating myself, and now co-authoring our book combine to help us move forward daily.

My journey with Paul as *a support person* is due to the Lord's pronounced promise to me years ago and my parents' role modeling, which helped me endure Paul's painful, scattered episodes. During the undiagnosed years, when neither of us grasped the underlying nature of his problems, he desperately sought life as a consistently fine man. We have remained soul mates on each other's team through thick and thin.

Paul's consistent dedication to take his meds is a sign of his love for me and our children. His medications are a godsend and help him manage his mental illness and disown an addiction scarred by recklessness and self-destruction.

Cheerleading Ideas! I Win, I Lose, Then I Go Forward Again!

I have gathered a list of ideas that help me as Paul's cheerleader and share them with you as tools while also recognizing that mental illnesses are unique to each person and situation: married, single, any age, family, friend, divorced, or engaged. One size does not fit all. Customize anything from this list for your own contexts, *your* givens. I haven't yet conquered my list, but even the act of trying and practicing the tools has been impactful. Value your fortitude!

> **Listen. Listen.** Above all, **listen**!
> **Use a calm voice.** Tough when conflict is brewing.
> **Quietly take a brea**k, go to another room, or walk.
> **Be kind to yourself.** Nourish your body, soul, and spirit.
> **Mutually agree on a plan** to navigate tensions.
> **A Duo of Words:** Thank you and please.
> **A Winning Trio:** Hugs, affirmation, and noticing progress.
> **A Quartet of Responses:**
>> Do you need to be alone right now?*
>> Thanks for letting me know.*
>> I love you no matter what!*
>> You are not your bipolar.*

I found a helpful article in *BPHope* called "10 Things Not to Say to Someone with Bipolar" by Tanya Hviliizky. I've learned and am learning what *to* say, yet it is equally helpful to learn what *not* to say. It has opened great conversations between Paul and me about what's specifically helpful to him on both ends of the spectrum. You can use this article as a conversation starter between you and your loved ones as well.

Bible Verses to Soothe the Soul

I experience the Bible's ancient words as a lasting remedy for stress, providing wisdom and hope. I keep these verses at the ready to remind me of God's faithfulness. Here are some of my favorites.

Psalm 34:18: "The Lord is close to the brokenhearted and saves the crushed in spirit."

Psalm 23:4: "Even though I walk through the darkest valley, I will fear no evil, for you are with me; your rod and your staff, they comfort me."

Isaiah 43:2: "Do not fear, for I have redeemed you; I have summoned you by name; you are mine. When you pass through the waters, I will be with you; and when you pass through the rivers, they will not sweep over you. When you walk through the fire, you will not be burned; the flames will not set you ablaze."

Matthew 11:28: "Come to me, all you who are weary and burdened, and I will give you rest."

1 Peter 5:7: "Cast all your anxieties on him because he cares for you."

Yes, we have scars. Our adult children have scars. Occasionally, a scar flares up. Nevertheless, forgiveness is a motif that God has firmly embedded into our family. A dear friend once remarked, "Arlene, you and your family have taught me how to forgive." God deserves 100 percent credit for making forgiveness possible.

Although Paul is eighty and I am seventy-eight, glancing back over the decades, I am still frankly astonished. We have lost friends who found it difficult to be with us in our brokenness, and we are deeply grateful to friends who have stood with us in our sorrows and loved us in our brokenness. Paul and I often remark, "The Lord's unconditional love for us, despite ourselves, is utterly amazing." In the valleys of the shadows of death, our Good Shepherd has anointed our heads with oil and favored us with goodness and mercy. He gave us two precious infants in our forties through adoption. He opened opportunities to serve Him as missionaries and professional staff with seven different Christian and Jewish organizations between us. We launched several successful businesses and have enjoyed many unusual and exciting adventures at home, living on a Mercy Ship and in Switzerland and Romania, and frequent trips to Israel, our spiritual homeland. The Lord is a faithful Friend, a wise Counselor, and a cherished Comforter by our side in our darkest and brightest moments.

> *"The will of God is never exactly what you expect it to be. It may seem to be much worse, but in the end, it's going to be a lot better and a lot bigger."* —Elizabeth Elliot

> *"I can do all things through Christ who strengthens me."* —Philippians 4:13 (my life verse)

Chapter 6

Questions We Ask Each Other

As co-author of *Mental Health Meltdown* with my wife, Arlene, I also serve as a co-facilitator of two bipolar in-person meetings, which meet at our church, part of a national organization called Depression and Bipolar Support Alliance (DBSA). In addition, I frequently interact in several online groups where I often post interesting questions and ask permission to share answers in The Voices of Bipolar Facebook group, which I created and host. This page was an instrument to gather the stories of those who have bipolar and other mental illnesses, many of which are featured with permission in chapter two. I asked the group four questions for chapter six, which provide first-person insights into varied opinions about how those with mental illnesses think and feel. I indicate male (M) or female (F) in the responses.

Question 1: Do you think bipolar is a curse?

- I feel like this is something we must go through so we can better ourselves and help others. (F)
- There are gifts, too. We can love deeper. Have creativity. Empathy. We are beautiful and unique human beings but sometimes, it does feel unfair. It's hard, but we can feel emotion bigger than most people. Sometimes joy, sometimes pain. (F)
- Yep. It cost me my marriage. (M)
- Every day, I wonder what I did wrong to have this. (M)
- No, I feel like it's a demon or two, maybe three to five, LOL. My husband loves me more than my demons do, and he

helps me come out of my episodes with compassion and patience. (F)

- It is a blessing in many ways. I have a much bigger heart and care more, which benefits me because I've been in nursing for thirty-plus years. It makes each of us special in our own way, and we have to figure that out. (F)
- No. Most people who have bipolar are intelligent, witty, charming, creative, and funny. It's how you play the cards you're dealt. (F)
- Sometimes, plus the manic episodes, voices/music, and other things are terrible. (M)
- Yes, and I have passed it on to my children. (F)
- Definitely. Even though I don't believe in curses, I make an exception in this case. It's fu**ed. (M)
- I decided that I would never have children, not that I really wanted them. It solidified my decision since I did not want to take the chance that they would suffer like I do. (F)
- I think bipolar is a curse. All it has brought me is self-doubt after the mania, financial problems, and sometimes criminal stuff. It cost me my marriage and freedom, but I now have sobriety and med compliance. It is the only way for me to move forward, even if I must live in a sober living house with many restrictive rules as a forty-two-year-old adult starting life over. (M)
- I sometimes feel that it is a curse, but then I am fascinated with the brain. We are really in a frontier land when it comes to the brain. (F)
- It's a gift for me because I found my true calling to help others because I understand what they're going through. (F)
- Yes, my entire life took a turn for the worse. I lost my teaching career, rights to my son, my husband, and family because of a two-year manic psychosis. (F)

- Sometimes, it's special, too, depending on the mood, but I know for a fact that bipolar took me places I wouldn't have visited without it. (M)
- It's a lifelong prison sentence. (F)

Author's Summary

The question about bipolar as "a curse or not" was poignant. Some gave answers based on religious beliefs, others based on suffering in relationships, jobs, friendships, pain, and even a few who recognized the positives of having bipolar. At eighty years old, with bipolar all my life, I could easily answer from any of those perspectives. None of them are right or wrong. I hope what I have chosen encourages all of you.

I choose to appreciate the sun rising and to walk in its colors. I choose to gaze on a full moon and its celestial companions. I choose to fight against the cycles of bipolar and depression that invade my life. I choose to live aware that some days are better than others and that I have the gift of life. I choose to love my life and make the very best of it, whether my days are in total wellness or the worst of bipolar. I choose to comfort those in my life. I choose to appreciate my wife's unconditional love for forty-eight years. I choose to live.

Question 2: When is the right time to share about your mental illness, and in how much detail?

- I don't share anything! When I have, people back off, not understanding. My ex-husband left, and I can't undo my actions. (F)
- My medical history and diagnosis are my personal business, and no one has the right to that information. (F)

- It's usually in my best interest to keep my mental health outside of the workplace. As for personal relationships, the "right time" is when I feel comfortable sharing. (F)
- I let employees know during the interview. I let friends know when they become good friends. I let my wife know as soon as I found out. (M)
- I let people know once they spend time knowing the real me and not a person with an illness. Some people can't look past it at first. (M)
- As an ex-girlfriend of a bipolar person, once the relationship gets exclusive, you should tell. My ex never told me, and I went through emotional pain because I did not understand what was going on. I sacrificed everything and went across the world for him. He never told me about his bipolar, but his mother did, and then he cut me off completely. (F)
- I don't hesitate to tell people, but the time must be right. I don't just blurt it out and say, "Oh, by the way, I'm bipolar." On a vacation, I had a conversation with a woman, telling her I have bipolar. It was a positive experience, and she asked me to explain it, which was hard to do. Nobody asked me in the way she did. I thought it would be easy knowing so much about it, but it's not. I found a great article later and sent it to her and learned that her daughter was recently diagnosed with bipolar. Our conversation was such a positive experience because it gave her a safe place to talk about what they were going through. I'm an RN, and it's important for people to know that we are intelligent and lead productive, happy lives. It's the only way to stop the stigma of our disorder. (F)
- With new friends and new romantic relationships, I tend to tell right away. I told my current boyfriend within twenty minutes of the first time we hung out. I don't usually mention it on the job, although I've considered it in my most recent job (so far, six months). I've had a lot of lows since then and have

considered telling them as a way for them to better understand why I am the way I am at times. (F)

- I'm blunt, so I tell people right away that I have been stable for over four years. Others had told me they thought I was bipolar for many years before I ever had a manic break or diagnosis. Full disclosure works best for me. If others have a problem, they don't need to be in my life. I'm also a grandmother of three and not looking for a mate. If the right one came along, I'd tell him. (F)
- Friends at my church know since it's part of my testimony. The setting must be confidential with people you can trust. Too many people label us without reason. It's complicated since bipolar is sometimes why I react in certain ways. A stigma surrounds it. (F)
- I am in a group, a safe place where we can complain among ourselves. We share the good times and the bad times with each other. I believe in speaking out, and I am not one bit ashamed or embarrassed about having bipolar. I'll tell anyone. I'm sixty-two, and one of my passions is education and helping end the stigma. (F)
- I only tell those I highly trust. I'm a self-employed teacher and don't want to risk anything. It's like physical health. I only tell what needs to be known when it needs to be known. Medical professionals, close family and friends, yes, not the world. (F)
- Old friends or doctors supporting me are easy. I take my best guess to their reaction and decide if it seems safe. In my last job, three others turned out to have it! I only share with those worthy. Ask yourself if there is a benefit or a detriment. It takes a lot of information to really understand this disease. (F)
- I tell co-workers early, ones that either supervise me or where we depend on each other because it affects my energy and organization. They should know that some days, I won't be as

coherent. My subordinates/staff do not know because it does not affect them or their duties. (F)

- Only my husband, grown son, and one of my grandsons. I don't see the need for anyone else to know. They understand and support me. (F)
- For me, as soon as possible. I've gone through various stages of stability, but I have been mostly stable for two years now. I am not ashamed or worried about being judged because I didn't choose to have bipolar. (M)

Author's Summary

Thanks to all who have shared your thoughts, experiences, and advice about the process you go through and the risks you do or won't take. Your answers describe the uniqueness of each person. I know that your voices in *Mental Health Meltdown* will help readers understand this aspect of sharing your mental illness.

Question 3: What are your absolute dos and don'ts to maintain a relationship between a bipolar and nonbipolar person?

- These are obvious, but I'll give it a go. Both need to understand the disorder and its symptoms and warning signs. Both must trust each other. Make an agreement that in times of doubt, the bipolar person is willing to listen and consider the non-bipolar perspective as more likely true. This agreement has saved us several times. I must trust he knows what's happening if my brain is lying to me. I also keep a therapist for weekly visits. Don't use it for excuses (for either person) or use the disorder as a weapon to hurt. (F)
- Communicate using non-violent styles. Educate your partner about bipolar disorder and educate yourselves. Read about

the bipolar spectrum and the positive qualities surrounding bipolar. Emphasize the importance of medication and honesty. Work together to problem solve. Create a crisis plan if suicidal thoughts or mania become apparent. Treat each other as equals. Remember your values and practice self-care-behaviors that don't involve your partner. Trust in love and remember that your disorder is just a small part of who you are; bipolar people can teach our non-bipolar partners, and we can learn from them. We are not defined by our disorder but by how we choose to view it. So, go out there and love wholeheartedly! (M)

- Be honest with the good and bad. Don't expect your partner to 100 percent understand and be unconditionally forgiving. Only someone going through it gets it. (F)
- Talk, talk, talk. Explain what you're feeling. Don't hide. If it's serious, they will want to know and can be a huge help. (F)
- As the bipolar person in my marriage, I take my meds and communicate! Tell my husband when I'm down and why. (F)
- We deal with the storms when they come. We live our best life as much as possible, refusing to let it beat us. (F)
- Communication, compassion, support, empathy, patience, compliance with their treatment plan, and willingness to try maintaining healthy behaviors even if falling into old patterns. Understand that neurodivergence leads to behaving differently on a baseline because of their illness. (M)
- Be fully honest and unafraid about your condition and your state at any given moment. If someone can't be supportive, they are not the one. My husband learned everything he could about my bipolar and schizophrenia disorders. He sees changes in me and knows what to do. I communicate everything to him so I can get the support I need. Do not feel like your diagnosis is something to be ashamed of, and don't hide your symptoms. (F)

- Create a crisis plan. Do your therapy as needed. Take your medication. Trust each other. Be willing to do couples therapy as needed. (F)
- Don't let our moods affect you too much. Do find ways to support us in treatment, meds, and a routine that works for us and helps us stick to it. Do let us know if you see a mood or behavior shift. I don't always realize when I'm slipping into an episode, but my husband sometimes sees the signs. (F)
- Make bipolar as small as possible in all relationships. Don't use significant others as a therapist. People get overwhelmed if we do so. I lost some friends, and I can't blame them. I was too much to handle for anyone. When I'm doing badly, I'll give my husband a heads-up that I'm struggling. He always offers support if I need it. I have a therapist to go unload everything instead. (F)
- Just being able to say, "I'm not okay mentally right now," and for the other person to have empathy. That means the most to me. Just allowing me to go through my stuff. (M)
- Communication both ways: keep God in the center of the relationship, encourage healthy habits and routines, and understand both parties will mess up and get their feelings hurt. Don't expect perfection in your partner or expect them to read your mind. (F)
- Bipolar can challenge any relationship, but we must understand that our illness can be difficult for our loved ones to manage. If possible, offer the loved one the opportunity to learn how to know your early warning signs. We must be responsible for our own illness, too, so we do everything required to manage our illness and learn our own warning signs. Communicate and don't assume. Be honest about our illness and how it affects us. No point leaving it all to surprise. It is our responsibility to manage our illness, and our partner can become part of that. (F)

Author's Summary

I observe stories here about marriages without a bipolar partner, which offer great suggestions to share a closer relationship of love and forgiveness for any couple. Thank you for your proactive ideas about living with a bipolar person. You give readers the strength to devote their all to their loved one or the courage to leave for their own survival and that of children if necessary.

Question 4: Why do people say, "I am bipolar" and not "I have bipolar"?

The way we speak and think about ourselves has a positive or negative effect on our quality of life. In the mental health world, the same holds true, perhaps more significantly. Like the three previous questions, I notified the group as follows: "This conversation is one that will help others understand how we refer to ourselves and our bipolar challenges when added to *Mental Health Meltdown*. All your responses are anonymous unless you choose to declare yourself."

- Because it's something I can't control, and it's not something I have; it's something I literally am. (F)
- I am bipolar. Just like I am a woman, and I am white, and I am educated, and I am funny, and I am a mother, it's part of who I am, and I can't separate it from my being; I don't have it: I am it. (F)
- My statement is never the same. I am not my illness. But my illness still influences my life. I've learned, I've acquired, and I've overcome so much. It is fair to still say "am" because it is part of my everyday life, even if I'm stable with treatment. Why? Because at any point, things could change, and I become manic or depressed, or a few smaller symptoms appear. Because of the humor, knowledge, routines,

preparations, thought processes, techniques, and types of therapies that I've picked up, the disorder remains. It shapes the person I am, yet it doesn't own or control me. The first part still tends to "am," while the last part is a personal reminder and acknowledgment so that I don't go into a victimhood mindset. (F)

- Often, to those who don't know me, I say "I have" first to establish that it's a diagnosis. Afterwards, or for those who know me, I say "my bipolar" if I'm talking about symptoms outside of them happening. If they are presently happening, then I say, "I'm bipolar," and then "my bipolar" in further explanation.
- My relationship with this disorder is my own. Everyone experiences it differently. It may be the same diagnosis but we do not experience symptoms or deal with it the same way. It is subjective, and thinking of the bipolar person first is respectful. (F)
- I say, "I have bipolar," because it gives me power over the mental illness instead of succumbing to it. (F)
- I have bipolar. I am NOT bipolar. It does not define me. Therefore, I AM NOT bipolar; I *have* bipolar. It does not define me; not everyone who knows me knows that I have bipolar. (F)
- The "don't let your label define you" crowd can damage people. Talk about your own mental illness how you want, but don't police how other people talk about theirs. Everyone is different; for some people, claiming their label is vital to recovery. (F)
- I feel like bipolar regulates my personality. It's a part of me. I AM bipolar. Also, "bipolar" is an adjective. You wouldn't say, "I have autistic."

- I say, "I am bipolar," because, for me, it took the stigma away and allowed me to find a path to live with it rather than suffer from it. Granted, it is the absolute worst roommate! LOL. (M)
- I say, "I have a neurological disability," since I found that people don't react well to "bipolar." I said that for the first year, and it didn't go well. Now, if asked, I say, "I have a neurological disability." (F)
- Because it is all-consuming and dictates every part of my life, I feel like nothing but a disorder, so I say, "I am bipolar." (M)
- I meet people who have Stone Age mentalities. If I say, "I have bipolar," many times they say, "When are you going to get rid of it or overcome it?" Or the more common, "Are you still on your meds?" I then say, "I am." (M)
- I say, "I suffer from bipolar disorder." I feel it makes it more acceptable as a disease than just being "crazy." (F)
- I say, "I have bipolar," because it doesn't define me. It's just a part of me. I have blonde hair; I am not blonde hair. I have green eyes; I am not green eyes. I have bipolar; I am not bipolar. I am not my illness. I *am* artistic; I *am* kind and considerate. (F)
- Why not use first-person language and say, "I am living with bipolar disorder"? (M)
- I suffer from moderate to severe bipolar disorder. (F)
- My therapist suggested, "I am a person who experiences bipolar." (F)
- I have bipolar disorder, and my wife suffers from it. (M)
- I know the secret; don't say anything at all. Problem solved. Has worked for me for years. (F)
- I like to say, "I live with bipolar disorder." (M)
- We need a good amount of self-compassion practice! (F)

Author's Summary

I prefer to say, "I have bipolar." I'm diagnosed with good meds, and while I cannot stop the presence of this brain disease, I can control what I allow it to do to me. Mental and physical illnesses happen, and both need treatment. It is a brain disorder I have; IT IS NOT WHO I AM!

Chapter 7

A Little Encouragement Goes a Long Way

My wife, Arlene, and I were visiting with a long-time close friend who is like a sister. She knew I had joined bipolar groups and asked if I shared any of my poetry with them. I answered, "I have not, but I do write words of encouragement now and then." She asked me to read a few to her. I did, and she responded, "That's really encouraging, Paul. You should use it and others in the *Mental Health Meltdown* book." I looked over at my bride and our dear friend, Susan, who shares my birth date. I listened. So, here they are. Thank you, dear friend.

I've shared many times in many groups. There are one hundred-plus variations of bipolar and mental illness support groups on Facebook: places frequented by the newly diagnosed, those who feel misdiagnosed, those seeking to discover if they have a mental illness, families with bipolar members desperate to understand, and those who are veterans in their ongoing struggles. Often, it is an agonizing cry for understanding and companionship. Many speak about love, and love lost relationships or friends and family abandoning them because they did not understand and/or tolerate their behaviors. Even with professional therapy available, much more is needed than an hourly visit. A myriad of questions are asked and answered by peers of all ages who have experienced the same situations. Decisions to live another day are made thanks to responses of encouragement and empathy.

At eighty, I still gain more understanding about having bipolar and find that I am helpful to some, mostly younger and newly diagnosed folks who, because of my white hair and age, seem to value my input. There are a few oldies like me who appreciate having senior fellowship. It is my privilege to help, but I, too, value the camaraderie of my fellow survivors. Sharing some of my comments in Facebook groups, I hope you will receive a bit more insight into our lives with bipolar, depression, anxiety, PTSD, and other mental illnesses. I am blessed by my readers to be a blessing, willing to reach out with words that help someone get through the day. If you know someone who has any mental illness, I hope my thoughts will help you.

A Prose Look at Living with Bipolar

My eyes open, daylight surrounds me, but my mind is in darkness. My emotions, spirit, and will are all in this darkness. It is a strange darkness, but I am not a stranger to it. I start most days here. I am closed in, cannot, will not, and don't even want to try to escape this darkness. My only regret in these moments is that I can feel it, and I don't want to. I am in a coffin deep underground; the daylight cannot reach me. My physical self rises reluctantly, climbs into clothing, trying to kick-start the day. I hear my soulmate attempt to reassure me as we take our morning walk. We talk about the highlights of our life, gratefulness for our marriage, and her appreciation of me. My spirit begins lifting but is unable to push through the lid of the coffin. "Help me," my spirit cries out to awaken my *will*. "Help me out of here!" Acting in response to the cry, *will* pushes the heavy lid off.

The flow of dirt and light surrounds me; emotions cry out, "Leave me alone; let me be!" I feel my *will* say no to emotions. *Will* begins the climb, digging up, and spirit joins in. Breaking to the surface, *will* decides to go for the day; spirit is smiling and soaring. Emotions want to crawl back into the dark to cover up and be left alone. I force my emotions to pay attention to: "It's not about how I feel." Emotions scream out, "It is! It's about me. I have nothing to enter this day for." But *will* and spirit continue until emotions either join in the day or just quietly endure. Then,

I am free to live another day in the sunshine of life. That is what it was like before diagnosis and medication. I thank God for a proper diagnosis and treatment. I encourage you, if your days begin like mine, to get diagnosed and treatment and freedom!

I Want Out!

In honor of The National Alliance on Mental Illness (NAMI) Suicide Prevention Month, I am reposting what I have shared in numerous groups when someone was indicating, "I want out" or "I want to stop." Some say it was helpful. I hope it will help you, too. Please feel free to pass it on:

Bipolar is a yoyo of emotions, a scream that has no end, a thrill higher than a kite can fly, a fall that has no end, and feelings that have no treatable cause. When I am down, there is no bottom, and when I am up, there is no limit. Bipolar is a merry-go-round that has no golden ticket to capture.

I want out! This is for everyone who wants life to stop! We all want out! Out of feelings that will not stop. Out of being and feeling different. Out of screaming. Out!!

Let's face it, right now, there is no good out! But tomorrow? Tomorrow, the feelings may be less, the screaming may not be necessary, a friend may finally understand. I may be able to help someone who needs out, too!

There is a voice that is telling you how to make it stop! Do not listen to that voice! It's not you! It is the enemy of your soul. This enemy is a liar! If you listen to that voice, you will not have a tomorrow, a chance at a good day, or just a little better day. And everyone who loves you will think it was their fault, that they didn't show you enough attention or love, or didn't call you for a visit. And more. They will always feel cheated out of your love and friendship.

I know this because forty-six years ago, a friend found me bloody and cleaned me up. All who heard about my "almost" thanked me for choosing to live and live life with them. Yes, especially my bride of forty-seven years. I still have days when I want everything to STOP, but I won't choose to let my feelings cheat me out of what may come tomorrow, whatever it brings. Tomorrow is for all of us who choose to see it. Choose life, for those in your life who love you.

People talk about champions of all sorts.

Today, I want to talk about the champions of the mental illness community—the Real Champions of bipolar, depression, PTSD, and other challenges. Folks who take their medications as an act of love to their spouse and family endure the fact that the medication often limits the full range of what they used to feel.

They create routines that enable them to be alert when symptoms begin, allowing them to have control over their actions regardless of the feelings that the medication can't control. They recognize that mental health, as with physical health, requires living with change. Their families, too, are champions of love and commitment—recognizing their loved one is dealing with a genuine health situation in the best way possible. You, too, can become a champion. Acknowledge that mental health deserves the same care and concern as any physical health situation.

Mental illnesses are difficult, yet they could be worse.

The other night, a singer named "Nightbird" sang on *America's Got Talent* and won the gold ticket, which was another opportunity to compete. Not only was her song lovely, but then she shared that she had cancer and was given six months to live. Her husband ran out on her when she was diagnosed, and her latest results gave her a 2 percent chance to survive. When Simon, the famous judge, said, "That is tough," she replied, "Two percent is nothing. It's something, and you can't wait until life isn't hard anymore to be happy."

Layers of Healing!

In my bipolar journey, I have found that healing comes in what I call "layers of healing," not in a big instantaneous way where every issue goes away permanently. It is one step at a time, and I am still learning.

The Five-Hour Drive Home

I was full of awareness that I had not enjoyed in a long time. I was simply happy to be on the road with my bride, Arlene. On the way to church the next day, I was aware that my emotions were filled with the enjoyment of Arlene's presence seated next to me. I silently praised God for my joy of answered prayer. When a negative occurs, I can identify it more quickly and choose not to allow bipolar to assume control. This is truly a REAL MIRACLE born and maintained in prayer. Yes, there are days I must fight for joy even though I want to scream. Recently, our son's dog ate all the hamburgers I left defrosting on the counter. I chose to laugh about it and pulled out other frozen burgers to defrost. These may not seem like huge events, but added layers of healing, big and small, have helped me more successfully make healthy choices. I hope the same goes for you. Be unafraid to find a few friends you trust, who listen, and who will support you.

With Independence Day Celebrations

I am so glad to live in the United States. My parents immigrated here through Ellis Island when they were children, so I'm a proud first-generation American! Serving in the Navy, I have years of good memories of the whole country celebrating together regardless of political beliefs. Millions of us face these mental health challenges. I have traveled to many countries, both first and third world. In poor countries, the education and treatment of any mental disorder is not available. In America, we have the world's best medical advantages and medications. I am celebrating all of YOU on July 4. Nothing anywhere is like support from each other.

Arlene's Author Summary

Helping you hold on to hope has underpinned the first-person stories and encouragement in *Mental Health Meltdown*.

I especially love quotes and included a few that may inspire you to take your next steps after reading our book:

> *Forgiveness is not an occasional act. It is a permanent attitude.* —Martin Luther King Jr.

> *Hope brings comfort to our aching souls. It perseveres, persuades, prevails.* —Billy Graham

> *Courage doesn't always roar. Sometimes courage is the quiet voice at the end of the day saying, 'I will try again tomorrow.* —Simone Biles, world famous gymnast

> *Trust in the Lord with all your heart and lean not on your own understanding; in all your ways submit to him, and he will make your paths straight.* —Proverbs 3:5–6

Educational Resources to Explore

Anxious Nation — The award-winning documentary exploring anxiety: https://anxiousnation.com/

WhiteFlag: the first mental health app with immediate customized peer support. WhiteFlag is a peer-to-peer-based messaging experience: https://www.whiteflagapp.com

The Mayo Clinic has extensive professional details and treatment information on bipolar disorder and more. Bipolar Disorder—Symptoms and Causes—Mayo Clinic

Paul's favorite video explaining bipolar disorder on YouTube by Dr. Domenick Sportelli, a double board-certified psychiatrist, titled: "What Is Bipolar Disorder?" (Bing Videos) He also recommends TEDx videos of people sharing their stories. Three are listed here. (Click through the ads):
- Surviving with a Mental Illness | Eric Walton | TEDxBoise | YouTube
- Finding Balance in Bipolar | Ellen Forney | TEDxSeattle |
- YouTube
- From Broken to Blessed on the Bipolar Spectrum | Sara Schley | TEDxDeerfield | YouTube

Weekly, free *BPHope* newsletter. Sign up at: www.mailbag@bphope.com

"Just Diagnosed? 5 Questions to Ask Your Doctor about Bipolar Disorder" | BPHope.com by Tanya Hviliitzky

National Organizations:

The National Alliance on Mental Illness

The National Institute of Mental Health (nih.gov)

Overcoming Self-Stigma in Bipolar Disorder (ossibd.com)

DBSA Depression and Bipolar Support Alliance (dbsalliance.org)

The film *Brainstorm* is an unprecedented initiative that combines inspiring stories of people with experiences of bipolar, cutting-edge science, and breakthrough treatments in one coherent narrative. https://brainstormthefilm.com/

Jade Zora Scibilla, www.BpHope.com (November 2023) lists eight movies and series streaming:
- *Queen Charlotte: A Bridgerton Story* (Netflix)
- *Modern Love* (Amazon Prime Video)
- *Spinning Out* (Netflix)
- *All the Bright Places* (Netflix)
- *Lady Dynamite* (Netflix)
- *Inside Out* (Disney+)
- *Touched with Fire* (Amazon Prime Video)
- *Kissed by God* (Amazon Prime Video)

Other Books by Paul Samuels

See tapestrypublishing.com and www.paulsamuels.com

Bipolar Missionary: Healing the Past, Shaping the Future

Expressions of Life: A Journey of the Emotions through Poetry

Children's Books:
- *The Rainbow Kids Find the Real Pot of Gold*
- *SUPPOSE*—A chapter book about liking yourself
- *Where Is Christmas?*—A chapter book for children

Paul Samuels Originals—Old Fashioned Parchment Greeting Cards — Emotions you can send or frame. Zazzle.com

Arlene Bridges Samuels

Weekly feature columnist for The Christian Broadcasting Network Israel. Access all her CBN columns at https://cbnisrael.org/category/arlene-bridges-samuels

About the Authors

Calling South Carolina home, Arlene Bridges Samuels' parents owned Universal Decorators, a professional parade float building company. Her early life in parades was full of happiness for thousands of families lining southern streets.

Growing up in a Baptist church, Arlene was active in choirs and youth groups. She has sung in many capacities as a worship leader, a professional folk singer, and as the owner of Southern Onion Singing Telegrams on Hilton Head Island, South Carolina.

In addition to serving as ministry staff with Young Life, Arlene was director for a Refugee Resettlement ministry and worked with Mercy Ships for eight years.

In her forties, she and her husband, co-author Paul Samuels, adopted two infants, their son in the US and their daughter in Romania. For the last twenty-five years, her work has included advocacy for Israel through Israel Always, the American Israel Public Affairs Committee, and the International Christian Embassy Jerusalem USA.

Since 2020, Arlene has been the weekly feature columnist for The Christian Broadcasting Network Israel.

Paul Leon Samuels is the son of Jewish refugees who escaped from the Russian pogroms under the czar. Born in South Bronx, he is a proud first-generation American. The pain and challenges of his early life have given birth to his creative writing through poetry and books, as well as public speaking.

Navy service on an aircraft carrier brought travel and discoveries. Though born in New York, Paul discovered the South and married southern beauty (and co-author) Arlene, Miss Florence, South Carolina. In their forties, they raised their adopted children and traveled the world with numerous humanitarian ministries:

World Vision, Mercy Ships, and Messianic Jewish Alliance of America. Their service in Youth With A Mission placed them in Romania, the homeland of their daughter.

Their return to the States was also characterized by success, as Paul built and owned successful real estate licensing schools. Together, Paul and Arlene serve on the board of Violins of Hope South Carolina, a sponsor of large concerts and educational events featuring Holocaust-era violins.

Paul is a co-facilitator for peer-to-peer support groups, affiliated with the national Depression and Bipolar Support Alliance (DBSA).

If You Enjoyed Our Book, Will You Help Us?

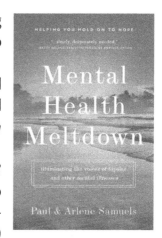

- The best way to recommend reading this book is WORD OF MOUTH, so please tell your friends.
- And your social media? Get on board with us for a digital train ride! Friend us on Facebook at *Mental Health Meltdown*.
- Are you a writer, blogger, podcaster? Have a website? Include the link to our website at *thementalhealthmelt-down.com*. You may cite up to 150 words.
- POST A REVIEW on Amazon, Goodreads, Facebook, X/ Twitter, Telegram, YouTube, and Instagram.
- ADVOCATE by suggesting us for interviews, both in person or via Zoom. We love conversations!
- SHARE the Facebook group, The Voices of Bipolar, at this QR code on the right: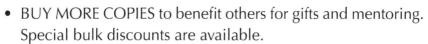
- Ask your bookstore to carry *Mental Health Meltdown*.
- BUY MORE COPIES to benefit others for gifts and mentoring. Special bulk discounts are available.
- Host a book launch party at your home, church, or small group.

We invite you to interact with us via our email newsletter, blog, public speaking, and social media group forums. Reach out via the contact form on our website at *thementalhealthmeltdown. com*.

Arlene Bridges Samuels is also a weekly columnist for The Christian Broadcasting Network Israel (https://cbnisrael.org/category/arlene-bridges-samuels). This QR code links to her devotionals, published at www.ArleneBridgesSamuels.com.

We invite you to read our other books, too!

Paul Samuels

Bipolar Missionary: Healing the Past, Shaping the Future by Paul Samuels (2020, 160pp)

Paul explores his past in the South Bronx and beyond. Living with undiagnosed bipolar, finally, an answer! Harnessing his mental illness and addiction, he chose to share hope with others. What others say: *"Paul is a courageous survivor. He tells his story with brutal honesty and yet somehow with grace and forgiveness. Paul, thank you for your transparency, borne out of a sincere effort to help others."*

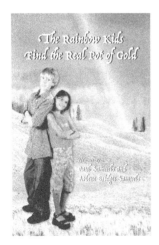

The Rainbow Kids Find the Real Pot of Gold by Paul Leon Samuels and Arlene Bridges Samuels (2019, 33pp)

People Kids go on a rainy-day adventure and reclaim the rainbow. What others say: *"My visiting seven- and ten-year-old grandchildren enjoyed it so much that I bought the book for gifts. Meaningful life lessons throughout the book are an added plus!"*

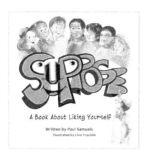

SUPPOSE by Paul Leon Samuels with illustrations by Linn Trochim (2017, 32pp)

Paul steps into the Seuss genre with a rhyming, fun-filled poem. Illustrator Linn Trochim adds full-color sparkle, drawing famous characters for Hanna-Barbera Studios. Children discover what they are SUPPOSED to do after a chase by a mischievous clown-kid. What others say: *"Paul's creative mind spills over in a way that makes me wish I were a child again and have someone read* SUPPOSE *to me."*

Where Is Christmas? (2008, 52pp)

Woody Squirrel falls into a snow drift where he overhears two People Kids talking about Christmas. He rounds up his forest friends for a treasure search. Phew Skunk sneaks in, causing trouble, but Wise Old Owl sets the story straight. Includes a song and sheet music.

You can order these books on Amazon or visit our website: thementalhealthmeltdown.com.

Printed in the USA
CPSIA information can be obtained
at www.ICGtesting.com
JSHW062023260924
70388JS00003B/6